HOW THEY CAST IT

An Insider's Look at Film & TV Casting

By Rob Kendt

Gabrielle —
All best with
cast...
M... ...te
in a
...re book-

7/30/05

lone eagle

THE REPORTER

How They Cast It
An Insider's Look at Film & TV Casting
Copyright © 2005 Rob Kendt

LONE EAGLE PUBLISHING COMPANY
5055 Wilshire Blvd.
Los Angeles, CA 90036
Phone 323.525.2369 or 800.815.0503
www.hcdonline.com

Printed in the United States of America
10 9 8 7 6 5 4 3 2 1

Cover design by zekeDESIGN
Book design by Carla Green

Library of Congress Cataloging-in-Publication applied for

Books may be purchased in bulk at special discounts for promotional or educational purposes. Special editions can be created to specifications. Inquiries for sales and distribution, textbook adoption, foreign language translation, editorial, and rights and permissions inquiries should be addressed to: Jeff Black, Lone Eagle Publishing, 5055 Wilshire Blvd., Los Angeles, CA 90036 or send e-mail to info@loneeagle.com.

Distributed to the trade by National Book Network, 800-462-6420.

Lone Eagle Publishing Company™ is a registered trademark.

Casting notices have been provided courtesy of Breakdown Services, Ltd. All rights reserved.

From the Publishers of ▼**vnu** business media

Contents

Preface
Breakdown Services and Breakdowns
(...where it all starts to come together...)

When a casting director is hired, a creative and collaborative process begins that is either unknown or misunderstood by most individuals outside of the mainstream of the entertainment industry. "Breakdowns" are a starting point for the majority of casting directors. They are relied upon by casting directors as a way to communicate what type of actors they are looking for when they are casting an episodic television show, a pilot, feature film, commercial, reality show, theatre project, or student film.

The process starts when a casting director submits a script to Breakdown Services. A Breakdown Services staff writer reads the script and culls information about the characters created by the screenwriter or writers. This information is then organized into a "Breakdown" of the project's roles, which contains the physical information about each character as well as each character's mental attitude and how he or she interacts with other characters within the script. The Breakdown is created with a maximum of objectivity and a minimum of subjectivity; the goal is not to embellish on the screenwriter's vision but to hone and define it so that agents can quickly determine what roles are available and which of their clients might be best suited for them. Casting directors often contribute as well, creating their own descriptions for roles that are then released with the Breakdown.

Breakdown Services opened its doors in 1971 with the goal of streamlining the casting process and assisting casting directors in communicating their casting needs to talent agents throughout Los Angeles. Those were the days before personal computers, before fax machines, and long before the advent of the Internet. Then, a casting director would leave one script out for agents to read in the casting director's lobby. Agents and their assistants had to drive all over Los Angeles, read all the scripts they could, take notes on the roles to be cast, and then deliver or mail their suggestions to the casting directors in an expedient fashion. It was a frustrating, time-consuming, and tremendously inefficient process. When Breakdown Services first came along, agents saw it as a boon - finally, a way to save time and be able to access to more projects. Winning the trust of the industry's casting directors was another matter altogether; after several years of "trial by fire," Breakdown Services became a respected and necessary part of the casting industry.

After a Breakdown is released, agents submit pictures, resumes, and ideas to the casting director. The casting director then applies his or her own creative awareness of additional actors — who is available, how much do they want, what is the budget, who does the studio need to hire to fulfill a contractual commitment — all of these considerations play a part (and often play havoc) with the creative process. And what a process it is! Through it all, the casting director is the production's rudder, keeping the ultimate goal of assembling a cohesive cast as their primary objective. Many a career has been made through the determination of a casting director to convince the director to give a particular actor a chance. Many an award has been given for excellence to an actor when it is the casting director that fought tooth and nail for that actor over the objections of others. It has been said: "Fifty percent of directing is in casting." Sadly, only the television industry honors casting directors with an award. The Casting Society of America continues to push for more recognition, and maybe someday soon we'll see an Academy Award given for excellence in the field of casting.

With *How They Cast It*, we at Breakdown Services are hoping to open your eyes to the contribution that casting directors make to the filmmaking process. If you are a fledgling producer or director reading this book, you would be well advised to hire a casting director — and then listen to him or her! A casting director isn't just someone who calls in talent; a casting director makes your job easier by finding actors who can deliver the performances that will make your vision come alive.

—Gary Marsh, Peter Weiss
Breakdown Services

*For more information on Breakdown Services and
its many other sites for the entertainment industry, please visit:*

www.breakdownservices.com
www.actorsaccess.com
www.breakdownexpress.com
wwww.extrasaccess.com
www.realityaccess.com
www.showfax.com

Household "Friends" and Icons

Friends

Cheers' regulars had Sam's bar; the young singles of *Friends* had a coffeehouse, Central Perk.

While sitcoms set either in the home or the workplace have been commonplace since the beginning of television, and families and co-workers still form the *dramatis personae* for many of the most popular TV shows, from soaps to police procedurals, *Friends*, like *Cheers* before it, was an ensemble comedy in which unconnected urban singles essentially formed an alternative on-screen family.

Indeed, the title of co-creators Marta Kauffman and David Crane's series was initially *Singles*, invoking the underrated Cameron Crowe film about twentysomethings pairing up in Seattle. Charged with finding these eligible unmarrieds was Ellie Kanner, a former agent who'd gone on to assist with casting on the series *Dallas* and *Sisters*, and on her own had cast some independent features (*Sleep With Me*, *Kicking and Screaming*) and several pilots that hadn't been picked up.

Pilot season, 1994, was not shaping up to be a great one for Kanner; tied up with her job as co-casting director on the series *Lois & Clark*, which ran over its production schedule that year, she didn't have time to take a pilot at the beginning of the season (the network pilot season tends to run from January through mid-April).

What's more, Kanner wasn't necessarily the go-to person for sitcom pilots, and she had no special relationship with Kauffman or Crane. So what was it that landed her the *Friends* gig?

"Honestly, I think it was my availability," says Kanner with a self-deprecating laugh.

In fact, *Friends* came down the pike late that pilot season, which *did* suit Kanner's schedule. By the time she was free of her *Lois & Clark* commitment and *Singles* was seeking a casting director, most CDs were in the midst of their own pilots. The late Barbara Miller, who was then head of casting for Warner Bros. studios, called and offered Kanner the job.

"Once I read the script, I was thrilled to be doing it," Kanner recalls.

Not long after, on Mar. 3, 1994, the first Breakdown went out to agents and other talent representatives for the show, now titled *Friends Like Us*.

The "story line" listed at the end of the Breakdown didn't delineate a plot at all but instead offered a more ambitious and general outline, almost a mission statement, for the hit series to come: "A circle of twentysomethings grapple with financial difficulties and emotional entanglements as they struggle to establish themselves in the sometimes threatening and always highly competitive adult world."

What there was of the pilot's plot was instead conveyed within the Breakdown descriptions themselves: The instigating event is the sudden appearance of Rachel, the "adorable, spoiled, courageous" daughter of wealth and privilege who's just left her blueblood fiancé at the altar and shown up, in her wedding dress, on the Manhattan doorstep of her old high school friend Monica ("smart, cynical, extremely attractive"). Ross, Monica's "intelligent, emotional romantic" brother, perks up a bit at Rachel's arrival, since he had a crush on her in high school, though he himself is "still reeling" from a divorce in which his wife dumped him for another woman.

The rest of Monica's close friends, who tend to congregate at her spacious apartment as if it's an all-hours neighborhood diner, are her former roommate, the "sweet, flaky 'New Age waif'"

Phoebe; the "droll, dry...wry" Chandler, an "office drone;" and Joey, a "handsome, smug, macho" wannabe actor who lives across the hall.

Thus was outlined the basis of a small-screen ensemble that would become as immortal as the citizens of Mayberry or the denizens of Louie De Palma's hack garage.

GROWING UP WITH X

With networks scrambling for the past few years to find a replacement for the ratings bonanza that was the now-departed *Friends*, and the 18-35 demographic still entrenched as the most desirable to Madison Avenue, it's easy to forget that TV in the early 1990s hadn't yet produced a successful show about so-called "Generation X," the children of the baby boomers, sometimes also called "baby busters," who were at the time striking out on their own and finding their way in the "sometimes threatening and always highly competitive adult world."

This is the generation that embraced Starbuck's, Ikea, and the Internet—a generation of renters who gravitated to urban centers from New York to Seattle for the careers and the culture, putting off or redefining relationships and family, much as their parents had done in the 1960s, although for different reasons.

Friends was the first and—despite the success of such urban-set comedies as *Will & Grace* or *Just Shoot Me*—still the only long-running network sitcom that has reflected the attitudes of Generation X, and indeed essentially grown up with it, as its concerns turned from dating to childbirth and beyond.

That element of cultural zeitgeist certainly accounted for much of the show's runaway success, not only with audiences but with advertisers who wanted to reach and/or be associated with the urban-professional demographic portrayed on *Friends*.

But for casting director Kanner, there was no template for such a show in 1994. *Friends* wasn't a typical family or workplace sitcom, nor was it quite in the same brittle, edgy New York vein as shows like *Seinfeld* or even *Mad About You*. Whereas those shows were built around Jewish standup comics and their perspectives,

Friends was built around an ensemble—a young, attractive, and relatively hip ensemble at that.

And its version of New York was lighter, brighter, and, most significantly, somehow more universal than many Big Apple comedies. One can't imagine *Seinfeld* outside of New York, for instance, any more than one can picture Gilligan or Skipper in a walk-up apartment. But *Friends* took place in a sort of idealized urban setting that could have been Portland, Oregon; Studio City, California; or even almost any particularly lively college town in the U.S. (After all, there was something about the way all the "friends" would drop in and hang out at each other's apartments that comfortably recalled dormitory living).

Kanner, in short, had her work cut out for her. She took her cues from the script, and from producers Kauffman and Crane, who wrote the Breakdown character descriptions: This wasn't a show about quirky, outsized urban characters and their offbeat adventures so much as a show about young people navigating the limbo between college and mortgage, who would be, in a sense, coming of age together.

The actors she rounded up for "pre-reads" (auditions in which a large talent pool is called in to read with just the casting director) and then handpicked for network tests (harrowing, high-pressure live performances in front of a massed audience of producers and network executives) were almost all known quantities in Hollywood at the time, though not all had done three-camera sitcoms before. They reflected a mix of dramatic and comic actors that suited the series' mandate; all were actors, in short, who might have carried a non-ensemble series on their own.

First up was a performer known primarily for her comedy work, both as an improv and sketch comic at Hollywood's famed Groundlings Theatre and as a reliable sitcom staple. The previous season, in fact, Lisa Kudrow had been hired on the pilot of *Frasier* in the role of Roz, but was dismissed before shooting began.

"Lisa was the first [of the final cast] who came in and auditioned—she was, I think, my second audition," Kanner recalls. "Any casting director would have read the script and said, 'Oh my God,

Lisa Kudrow is perfect for [Phoebe].' I brought her in and we were ready to test her right away."

Kudrow came dangerously close to blowing the test, Kanner says, but the way she saved herself from oblivion offers an instructive lesson for actors.

"The day before we were testing, [Lisa] called and [said] she had a different take on the character, and asked if she could come in and show us what that take was.

"So she came in—I believe it was just Marta Kauffman and I— and did it completely different. It was just not Phoebe; I can't explain the specifics, it just wasn't. And we were like, 'No, no, no— do it how you originally did it.' And she was like, 'OK, fine.'"

The lesson: "As perfect as someone is for a part, if they come in and give a bad reading or they're off, you never know, they could lose the part. We didn't want that to happen with Lisa, because we wanted her to get the part. And she was smart enough to call and ask if she could come in and do it for us. I'm so glad she did that."

While there were relatively few changes made to the original character descriptions along the way (a reference to Chandler's craving for "snacks" was excised, lest agents thought they should submit only overweight actors for the part), there was one remarkable case of the producers, and Kanner, failing to recognize a casting choice which, in hindsight, seems obvious, even inevitable.

"Courtney Cox wanted to play Monica, but we wanted her for Rachel," Kanner says. "When she first came in, she read for Rachel and we loved her as Rachel. We wanted to take her to the network and have her test for Rachel. But she insisted she wanted to play Monica. I think she even came in and read for Monica, and we thought, 'Well, she was pretty good, but we still want her as Rachel.'

"So we finally relented and said, 'OK, you can come in and test at the network for Monica, if that's what you really want.' Secretly, we were going to offer her the part of Rachel afterwards. But then she came in and she was so great as Monica, we said: 'All right, she won it.'"

Ironically, Jennifer Aniston had also been mismatched initially: She was first called in to read for the part of Monica but asked instead to read for the part of Rachel. In her case there was no question, Kanner says.

"Jennifer came in and auditioned, and of course *owned* the part," Kanner recalls. "We loved her."

There was one big hitch, though: Aniston was already cast as a lead on a pilot for CBS, Barton Dean's *Muddling Through*, starring Stephanie Hodge as a white-trash mom returned from jail to her crazy family, including her daughter, played by Aniston. The show had bad buzz around town, and it was assumed it would not be picked up for the fall 1994 season.

"Lori Openden, who was the head of casting at NBC at the time, was in the process of making a backup holding deal for Jennifer, since everyone thought *Muddling Through* would go away," Kanner says. "Then we cast her knowing that *Friends* was in second position; first position was *Muddling Through*."

These "positions" refer to a common feature of the often fiercely competitive frenzy of pilot season, when networks vie for actors like they're sports stars (even before they're TV stars). As Lisa Miller Katz tells in the chapter about *Everybody Loves Raymond*, this competitive gamesmanship was a factor in the fast-track casting of Brad Garrett in the role of Robert.

In the case of Aniston, Kanner believes a competitive urge led CBS to pull rank.

"Apparently CBS heard about *Friends* when we shot the pilot [with Jennifer]. And I don't know if this is true or not, but they did pick up *Muddling Through*, when before then they weren't planning on it."

This left *Friends* and Aniston scrambling. While CBS allowed the actress to do both series, and *Muddling Through* didn't muddle through for long—it was finally cancelled after seven episodes, before the fall season even officially began—for a time in the summer of 1994, Aniston was possibly the hardest-working woman in show business.

David Schwimmer was not an automatic lock for the role of Ross, either. Showing his versatility, he had recently completed a meaty, dramatic multi-episode arc on *NYPD Blue*. And his experience the previous year on the short-lived Henry Winkler sitcom *Monty* had apparently soured him on the form.

"He actually passed when he read the script at first," Kanner recounts. "He didn't want to do another sitcom." But Kauffman and Crane, who had tested Schwimmer for a stillborn pilot the year before, "got on the phone and told him exactly what the role would be, and where the character was going, and convinced him to give it a shot. They changed his mind."

For the part of aspiring actor Joey, Kanner ended up championing the relatively unknown Matt LeBlanc, who hadn't even been submitted for the part by his agent at the time. Luckily, LeBlanc also retained a personal talent manager who was more attentive.

"Matt was probably the greenest of them all," Kanner concedes. "But every time he came in, he was better and better. And he's just the type of person you just fall in love with—he's charming, engaging."

Each time an actor was added to the ensemble, they formed a group that gathered to test with each new candidate. You'd think such group auditions would be routine in pilot casting, as casting directors are often putting together actors who have to form a believable family, or have some kind of "chemistry" together, but in fact they aren't very common at all. In the case of *Friends*, though, the aggregate approach obviously paid off.

"The last person we were casting was Matthew Perry," Kanner says. In a faint echo of Aniston's dilemma, he had just completed a pilot, *LAX 2194*, about baggage handlers of the future. To no one's surprise, it wasn't picked up, though that decision came perilously late. Perry was freed to read for *Friends* only at the last moment.

"He came in and read, we loved him, he went to the network, the rest is history," Kanner says. "When we went to the network, we had the rest of the cast there, so they were all reading scenes together. And when you saw that cast, you just thought, 'Oh, OK.' I mean, you could *see* the show. This was an ensemble from the beginning."

ICONS LIKE US

Among the criticisms that would later be levelled at *Friends*' idealized urban world was that it conspicuously lacked people of color, particularly (though, for a long while, not exclusively) among its leads. On the original Breakdown, hand-written notes saying "any ethnicity" were scrawled below the characters of Chandler and Phoebe. And Kanner says she read and considered many actors of color for several of the roles, but that the choices ultimately came down to "who was funny, who was right, and who fit, that's all."

Among the almost-rans who didn't make it on board the *Friends* juggernaut was Craig Bierko, best known for playing Harold Hill in the recent Broadway revival of *The Music Man*.

"We offered him the role of Ross *or* Chandler—he could take his pick," Kanner says. "But he decided to do a series where he was the star with a little kid—and you know, that could have been huge." Ironically titled *Best Friends*, that pilot wasn't huge—it wasn't even picked up. Says Kanner sympathetically, "Craig's a great actor, very funny. He would have been great in either role."

Among other actors who tested for Monica were Nancy McKeon, formerly of *Facts of Life*; Leah Remini, who now stars on *King of Queens*, and Tammy Lauren, best known since for roles on *Wanda at Large* and *Martial Law*.

These might-have-been *Friends* may have kicked themselves over the years—Bierko once good-naturedly quipped that the show he turned down "has replaced Christianity"—but it's a mark of felicitous casting that it is now impossible to imagine any other actors in those roles.

Ross, Rachel, Monica, Phoebe, Chandler, and Joey may have stood in for a generation, and their New York may have lacked a certain gritty specificity. But there was finally nothing generic about these six distinct, idiosyncratic television icons.

(File 3-B3) L
WARNER BROS. TELEVISION

"FRIENDS LIKE US"
1/2 HOUR PILOT/NBC
1ST DRAFT: MARCH 3, 1994

Executive Producers: David Crane, Marta Kauffman
Kevin Bright
Director: TBA
Writers: David Crane & Marta Kauffman
Sr. V.P. of Talent: Barbra Miller
Casting Director: Ellie Kanner
Casting Coordinator: Lorna Johnston
Starting Date: TBA
Location: L.A.

WRITTEN SUBMISSION ONLY TO:

ELLIE KANNER

Duplicate submissions (no pictures) to Barbra Miller at the above address.

[MONICA]   In her 20s, she's a smart, cynical and extremely attractive young woman who has had to work for everything she has. Monica is currently employed as an assistant chef at a chic uptown restaurant. A "romantic disaster area," she tries her best to play the dating game, but always winds up with deadbeats and losers. Bolstered by her close circle of friends, Monica still has high hopes of establishing herself as a successful adult, meeting Mr. Right, and going on to a sterling future. However, sometimes she has to wonder if she's just spinning her wheels in the same old rut...SERIES REGULAR (1) *[Copyright 1994, BREAKDOWN SERVICES]*

[RACHEL]   Monica's best friend from high school, Rachel is adorable, spoiled, courageous—and at the moment, just plain terrified. The pampered daughter of an extremely wealthy man, Rachel always had money to burn and no thought for the future. However, when she jilts her wealthy fiancé at the altar and incurs her dad's displeasure, Rachel shows up on Monica's doorstep in her wedding dress, looking for a shoulder to cry on. Although she is "equipped to do nothing," Rachel moves in with Monica and announces her intention of getting a job and turning over a whole new leaf—but her old spendthrift habits die hard...SERIES REGULAR (8) *[Copyright 1994, BREAKDOWN SERVICES]*

[ROSS]   Monica's older brother, aged 26, he's a professional paleontologist, and an intelligent, emotional romantic whose wife has just left him. Phenomenally reluctant to face "singlehood" again, Ross is still reeling from his wife's abandonment, not to mention the fact that she has just openly announced her lesbianism. Ross had a tremendous crush on Rachel in high school, and when she suddenly shows up on the scene, he starts taking a new interest in life once again. However, Ross's martial troubles aren't quite over, as he learns when his wife pays him a surprise visit and drops quite a bombshell on him...SERIES REGULAR (4)

[JOEY]   A handsome, smug, macho guy in his 20s who lives across the hall from Monica, he wants to be an actor. Actually, he wants "to be Al Pacino." He "loves women, sports, women, New York, women— and most of all Joey." A member of Monica's circle of pals, Joey is constantly hanging out at her place, bumming food, and kibitzing about her personal life. He thinks he's quite an expert on women, and is always hitting on new potential conquests...SERIES REGULAR (1) *[Copyright 1994, BREAKDOWN SERVICES]*

[PHOEBE]   A sweet, flaky "New Age waif," she's a good soul who sells barrettes on the street and plays guitar in the subway. Monica's former roommate, Phoebe still hangs out a lot with the rest of the gang. Actually, Phoebe has had a pretty rough life, but you wouldn't know it from her innate sweetness and naiveté. One of the world's worst songwriters, Phoebe performs her own atrocious compositions with hilarious flair...SERIES REGULAR (1) *[Copyright 1994, BREAKDOWN SERVICES]*

[CHANDLER]   Another member of Monica's circle of friends, he's a droll, dry guy in his 20s, a wry observer of everyone's life, especially his own. An office drone who "works in front of the computer doing something tedious in a claustrophobic cubicle in a nondescript office building," Chandler survives the grind by way of his "sense of humor. And snacks"—many of which he scores from Monica's refrigerator when her back is turned...SERIES REGULAR (1)

[PAUL]   A nice-looking, pleasant guy in his late 20s, he goes on a date with Monica. The two hit it off splendidly, and when Paul reveals that he is still traumatized from his recent divorce, and has not been able to perform sexually ever since, he arouses Monica's pity and interest. The two later have a torrid fling, after which Monica learns, to her fury, that Paul is handing her an embarrassingly transparent line to get her into bed...LEAD (17)

[FRANNY]   Monica's friend and confidante, this young woman chef works in the restaurant with her. Intimately familiar with Paul, she tips Monica off to the fact that she's been played for a bit of a fool...2 speeches & 5 lines, 1 scene (42)

[CAROL]   This woman in her 20s, Ross's soon-to-be-ex-wife, has recently announced her lesbianism and left Ross for her female lover. Now, she drops in on Ross at their old apartment to drop another bombshell into his life...4 lines, 1 scene (58) POSSIBLE RECURRING ROLE.

[WAITRESS]   This waitress serves coffee in the cozy coffeehouse where Monica and her friends hang out...1 line, 1 scene (9)

STORYLINE: A circle of twentysomethings grapple with financial difficulties and emotional entanglements as they struggle to establish themselves in the sometimes threatening and always highly competitive adult world...

Raising the Heat on "Raymond"

Everybody Loves Raymond

The deceptively average-looking CBS sitcom *Everybody Loves Raymond* has evoked many loving comparisons to its antecedents in the portrayal of the state of marriage in America, from *I Love Lucy* to *Mad About You*.

But casting director Lisa Miller Katz may be the first to liken *Raymond*'s successful formula to a slightly less exalted TV classic: *The Munsters*.

She's recalling the important left turn the *Raymond* casting process took back in 1996—introducing the WASPy, reasonable Patricia Heaton into the off-kilter suburbia of Ray Barone and his clingy Italian-American family.

"It makes her a little more Marilyn Munster," Katz says of Heaton's take on Debra, originally described by the writers as a "working-class knockout"—i.e., attractive but ethnically New York. "On *The Munsters*, Marilyn was the blonde, pretty one, and they treated *her* like the freak. So she's like, 'Why am I the one who feels out of place? You're all crazy around me, but I feel like I don't know what's the right thing to do.'"

What Katz is saying is startling, and not only because she's invoking a show that memorably featured a Frankenstein-style monster driving a souped-up hot rod. She's confirming something that seems almost unbelievable: that *Raymond*'s crucial ethnic/class conflict, between the sensible wife and her dysfunctional in-laws, wasn't even in the pilot script.

No mistake—there was conflict. Reading the original pilot Breakdown today, it almost reads as if Debra, not Raymond, is the lead character, navigating the slings and arrows of an outrageous family and getting little help from her passive husband.

The difference is that Romano and the show's co-creator, Phil Rosenthal, seem to have conceived Debra as holding her own against the formidable Barone clan in a more classically feisty vein.

"Talk about a working-class knockout—that's Leah Remini," Katz says of the lead in a family sitcom she would later cast, *King of Queens*. "She's very New York in her sensibility. She's not going to be messed with."

The other factor, of course, was the "knockout" part.

"Obviously from the beginning, I know they wanted someone who's good-looking," Katz explains. "'Working-class' kind of implies the New York flavor of what we were going for. We knew this family was gonna end up—or at least we were going to try make them feel—Italian.

"So, you say 'working-class knockout' and you make your list. In the beginning I was sort of going for—well, here's the Debra list: Amy Brenneman, Lisa Edelstein, and Maggie Wheeler, who now plays Debra's friend on the show, Linda. There was definitely an Italian flavor, prototypically, in what we were going for here."

Rosenthal was particularly sold on Wheeler's take on the role. But after a network test, CBS executives had the kind of response that told her her job wasn't done, Katz recalls.

"They said, 'Let's keep looking. And maybe she doesn't have to be so specific. Maybe we can widen our net a little bit here, and not just think that she has to match the Italian kind of New York flavor.'"

An agent's suggestion is what turned the tide.

"I was on the phone with ICM, and they said, 'What about Patty Heaton?' I said, 'That's a fantastic idea.' And within a day, we were sitting in the room with her, she read with Ray, and that was that. It was really one of those, 'Why didn't I think of that?' moments."

Apart from the contrast in background, Katz points out a few other things that cinched the deal.

"Patty is one of these actresses [where] I believe every single word that comes out of her mouth," Katz says. "I don't ever feel her acting; it never rings false. I just buy it. It's a real relationship."

What's more, Katz says, Heaton brought a reality to the part that couldn't be faked.

"She's a mom, too. And when she walked in the door for her first meeting, she had two kids at the time, and they were home with the sitter, so [she] was kind of like, 'OK, it's very nice to meet you, but my sitter has to be gone by three.' That's a real thing. And while that wasn't Debra on the page, that's life."

FORMULA ONE

The show's signature success is not all a case of casting serendipity, of course. As someone who's been the matchmaker for a number of marriage-and-family laffers—*King of Queens, According to Jim*—Katz is aware of the elements that raise *Raymond* a cut above the ordinary. And these were on the page from the start, she says.

"When you talk in terms of formula, it's: Wife says A and the husband does B," Katz says of the prototypical marital comedy of errors. Most sitcoms based on this model, she points out, simply conjure up the most extreme conflict they can, regardless of realism: "It's always, she wants him to do something and he's an *asshole*, so he does the most dicky thing possible. Sometimes there are elements of that [on *Raymond*], but...it's much more: Well, Ray's logic is this, and her logic is that. As opposed to, 'I'm just an idiot.'"

Creating a believable marriage is one thing—there has to be a kind of chemistry between the two leads, which, Katz says, can be "hard when you read two scenes with a person and you're supposed to base *everything* on that." Putting together a credible family from a group of unrelated, mixed-and-matched actors is also a challenge that takes sympathetic and careful casting.

How much, for instance, does physical resemblance play into assembling a family unit?

"Well, you have pictures on the wall and you kind of assemble it that way," Katz says. For Ray's brother, it was important he have "that same kind of olive coloring." Other than that, Katz insists, "It truly is about—thank God—who the funniest person is, who's right for the part, as opposed who looks the best for the part. Look at the kids—I got three blonde kids."

Audiences might be forgiven for not having noticed the kids in the first few seasons, as they were conspicuously absent from most of the show's scenarios.

"That was Decision One about this show: This is not a show about the kids," Katz says. "This is not *Full House*. This is about people who happen to have children, but the kids are not the props. And that's why a lot of episodes are like, 'Well, I just dropped them off at school,' or, 'They're down for the night.' It works."

In recent seasons, Katz admits, the kids have been featured more prominently: "In the episode we're shooting this week, Ally's thirteen and she's going to a party with boys and dancing. It's like, Jesus, [Madylin Sweeten] was *four* when we started this. It's been on for eight years! She's twelve, but she's playing thirteen. She was four when we cast her, and turned five before we started the episodes."

The actors chosen to play Ray's three immediate family members—brother Robert, father Frank, and mother Marie—were each distinct and inspired choices that were thoroughly hashed out by Katz and the producers.

Brad Garrett, the tall, sad-eyed actor with the surprising basso profundo voice who plays single policeman Robert with a kind of hilarious but touching gravitas, was not the obvious choice.

In fact, says Katz, "Brad's completely different than what we specified [in the Breakdown]. I brought Brad in because I had hired Brad once before, and tried to hire him a second time." The first time was on *Fresh Prince of Bel-Air*, the series on which Katz cut her teeth as a sitcom CD. The second time she tried to cast him, his height lost him the job: "I was casting *Space: Above and Beyond* for Fox, and I brought in Brad to play a guy who was trapped in a tank. They wanted to hire him, but the producers said, 'He has to be in a

tank the entire time; we think Brad would be too tall.' Brad is 6'8",
and he was in fact too tall."

But she didn't just think of Garrett because of past associations.

"I brought Brad in because I thought it would be a funny spin,"
Katz says. She and the producers had already considered a roundup
of usual suspects—actors who specialize in New York-y sidekick
roles: John Mendoza, Joe Pantoliano, Chris McDonnell, Chris
Moloney, Tom Sizemore, Anthony LaPaglia.

"We were really going for that, 'Hey, Ray, y'know, I'm your
brother.' They thought he would be a little schlubby, maybe a little
chubby, and a loser in that way. And then when Brad walked in the
door—that was kind of it."

Then came the hard part: Katz and the producers came up
against the fiercely competitive one-upmanship of pilot season, a
compressed few months at the beginning of each year in which networks play the zero-sum game of chasing a handful of coveted
actors, sometimes only because other networks are interested. It's a
time when actors can easily get their heads turned by the high
financial stakes involved, and by the temptation to play one bidder
off of another. In the midst of all that, it's almost easy for all con-
cerned to lose track of the ultimate goal: to put together a pilot that
will get picked up and have a long life on the air.

"During pilot season you're competing with all these other
pilots," says Katz. "An actor will leave your audition and you'll say,
'We wanna test him,' and [the producers will] say, 'Well, he already
has three test deals and he's going to go to network tomorrow for
The Hoo-Hah Show on NBC.' An actor has to decide who he wants
to put in 'first position'—which role he'd like more. A lot of times
it just comes down to, an actor just really wants a job, and so if
you're not going to the network for a week, and someone is going
to NBC the next day, they'll put NBC in first position and see if they
get that job. There's a lot of that."

Garrett, she recalls, was testing for "some fireman show" at Fox,
and it was a much better deal: a "pilot plus six," meaning that the
network had already ordered six episodes in addition to a pilot. "He
had the offer on the table to go test for the Fox thing; he preferred

our show, but we couldn't compete. I can't compete with a pilot plus six; that's money in the bank."

So some strings were pulled: The head of comedy casting for CBS, Michael Catcher, was a Garrett fan, and he took a tape of Brad's work—a number of sitcoms, including the gay lead in the short-lived *The Pursuit of Happiness*—directly to Les Moonves, the head of CBS. Moonves was persuaded, and authorized hiring Garrett immediately, without a network test. Under the circumstances, this was the only way to secure his involvement.

"Otherwise we risked losing him," Katz recalls. "The other show was still a what-if; he had to go test for it and book it."

PARENT TRAP

For the roles of Raymond's parents, Katz had a certain balancing act in mind.

"One of the things I felt really strongly about from the beginning of the pilot process was, I thought it was important for Marie and Frank to not outweigh, celebrity-wise, Ray and Debra," Katz says. "I didn't want them to come in and have the scales tip toward them. I wanted them to come in and be able to do their, 'We're going to come in, and we're going to wreak havoc on your house and say obnoxious things, and then we're gonna leave.' We talked about [celebrity] names for them for a long time, and I kept saying, 'I really think you should kinda go more this route.'"

Not that she went for unknowns. Indeed, after a lot of testing, the actors who eventually won the roles, Peter Boyle and Doris Roberts, were both on Katz's original lists.

Boyle, who had been a major character actor in the 1970s, had come to Katz's attention in an unlikely way.

"When I was doing *Space: Above and Beyond*, Glen Morgan was running the show, and he had been on *The X-Files*. So they sent me a rough cut of an episode that was gonna air in a few weeks; it's the one [Boyle] won the Emmy for. I watched it, and I totally fell in love with Peter Boyle again. I'd always been a fan.

"And so every meeting I went to that pilot season, I said, 'You should hire Peter Boyle.' I met someone on something, and I said, 'Who do you have in mind for the father?' and they said, 'We like

Paul Dooley, we wanna hire Paul Dooley.' 'Paul Dooley? He's played *everyone's* father on TV. Hire Peter Boyle.' I didn't get that job."

She already had the *Raymond* job when she again mentioned Boyle's name to Phil Rosenthal. And, as with Heaton and Garrett, a few meetings between Boyle and the producers were enough to convince them they'd found their Frank. Though other Franks were tested—including Victor Raider-Wexler and Len Lesser, who later recurred as Frank's buddies Garvin and Stan—the offer to Boyle came soon after he met with Romano and Rosenthal.

"I just thought it was just such a wonderful reinvention of him," says Katz of the casting choice. "You hadn't really seen him play this role before. He's a brilliant actor, and such an interesting man."

Indeed, it's probably the sense of a rough, untamed past that glimmers in Boyle's eyes, not to mention his crisp, almost peremptory delivery of Frank's often childish putdowns, that makes this TV patriarch uncommonly offbeat and maddeningly realistic.

As Ray's mother Marie, Doris Roberts expertly limns another parental type: the passive-aggressive, manipulative drama queen. It's a character just as recognizably real as Boyle's Frank, and it complements his dry detachment with its own wily entanglement.

According to Katz, Roberts herself exhibits a few of Marie's more self-dramatizing traits.

"Doris was on my original list, but she was hard to get in the room," recalls Katz. "She was very busy—she was directing a play or something. We'd been seeing a lot of people, and finally Doris showed up.

"I went out to get her in the waiting area. I said, 'Doris, are you ready? Come on, let's go in. I'm Lisa.' We're about to walk in the door, and she stopped me, grabbed me at the door, and she said: 'I'm just telling you right now: If I don't get this role, I'm tearing up my SAG card.' It was like, OK, no pressure or anything, but thanks! She's a hoot."

GROWING UP RAYMOND

When *Everybody Loves Raymond* premiered, it was not an immediate smash, but CBS allowed it to build momentum and a fan base, and the rest is history.

Though most TV critics were early advocates of the show, among the comparisons *Raymond* initially invited was to other standup-centered sitcoms, from *Roseanne* to *Seinfeld*. By that standard, it seemed at first that Romano might not be up to the task as a performer. An often expressionless cipher, Romano has a uniquely self-effacing presence for a TV star. Over many seasons, it has grown into a kind of individual style, but in that first season the meek Romano often seemed to barely register onscreen.

(Romano's affectless demeanor may be why he'd been fired the previous year after one day on the set of *NewsRadio*; his role as an electrician was taken over by Joe Rogan.)

"I think probably when he started the show, he was a much more shy person, and I think that read a lot in the first season," Katz concedes.

Did Katz get marching orders to surround this TV-shy comic with the most seasoned actors she could find, as has typically been the case with shows built around standups?

"That was never the directive with this: 'Oh, he's never done this,'" says Katz. "He was certainly green, but the seeds were always there. In the first few seasons, we had a coach [Richard Marion] who was with us every day on the stage. When Ray won the Emmy, he thanked him; he's since died. The learning curve was just amazing."

The show's curve—from everyday family sitcom to cultural icon, and to the Valhalla of endless syndication—has been no less striking, particularly to those involved in making it happen. Katz has seen great scripts fall apart in pilot production, great pilots not get picked up, and mediocre ones go to air. This show's happy ending began with a great script, by all accounts, but there were many places along the way that *Raymond* could have gone the way of the also-ran.

"Look, it's luck," Katz says. "*Everybody Loves Raymond* is lightning in a bottle. Getting a pilot is a miracle in and of itself, and getting that pilot picked up to air is a miracle in and of itself. We were on Fridays at 8:30 on CBS, the shittiest timeslot in the history of television. And still—in what world is this show still on the air? It's just a miracle. We were doing badly, no one watched us, no one knew who we were. We followed *Dave's World*.

"Les [Moonves] said, 'I kinda like this show,' and moved us around and put us on Monday night. It's a fucking miracle! You think about the odds, it's...it's staggering."

Katz shouldn't sell herself short, of course. If, as she says, "It starts with the word on the page, and this pilot script was hysterically funny," it's nevertheless true that matching the right cast to a such a script is an art form all its own. Katz's inspired casting choices have everything to do with what everybody loves about *Raymond*.

HBO INDEPENDENT PRODUCTIONS
IN ASSOCIATION WITH
WORLD-WIDE PANTS INCORPOTATED
"EVERYBODY LOVES RAYMOND"
HALF HOUR PILOT PRESENTATION/CBS
DRAFT: FEBRUARY 26, 1996

Executive Producer: Phil Rosenthal
Director: TBA
Writer: Phil Rosenthal
Casting Director: Lisa Miller
Casting Associative: Michael Testa
Start Date: Approx. 4/10/96
Location: Los Angeles

WRITTEN SUBMISSIONS ONLY TO: LISA MILLER

RAYMOND: CAST (RAY ROMANO)

NOTE: This half-hour pilot presentation is set Queens.

[DEBRA] In her mid 30s, A WORKING CLASS KNOCKOUT, Debra is happily married to Ray, a New York sportswriter. The mother of three, Debra is harried and drained by her three kids—but also by her three in-laws. Completely without privacy, intimacy, or respect, Debra is going rapidly insane, a result of the overbearing scrutiny and false bonhomie exhibited by her husband's chronically underfoot parents and brother. Tired of being held up for family scrutiny and slighting criticism, Debra pressures Ray to break away from his family a millimeter at a time, and finds her husband responding to her increasingly desperate pleas with a maddeningly overstated case of misplaced family loyalty...SERIES REGULAR (1) *[Copyright 1996, BREAKDOWN SERVICES, LTD.]*

[FRANK] Ray's father, Frank is a 60ish seasoned troublemaker who seems like an ardent family man, but is actually something of a nut. Frank has either never heard of the word "boundaries," or believes that they don't pertain to his happy family. Fond of his grandchildren, Frank loves to drop by and play with them, whether it's convenient for Ray and Debra or not, and he likes to stick his nose where it doesn't

belong: he cracked the code to Debra's answering machine and regularly monitors their calls, and thinks nothing of perusing Ray's phone bill—complete with comments. A man who (like his wife) regards Ray's apartment as a second home, Frank is invariably underfoot, oblivious to the fact that he is smothering Debra...SERIES REGULAR (24)

[MARIE]   Ray's mother, Marie is 60 years old and a busybody, yet she considers herself "refined." None too thrilled with her daughter-in-law, Marie regularly denigrates Debra's approach to homemaking and child-rearing, and drives Debra crazy by showing up at her home to criticize and carp. A woman whose life is thrown completely out of whack when Ray gives her the Fruit-of-the-Month-Club for a present, Marie seems expert at both playing the martyr and evading any fundamental change in life. Very very fond of her son (to the point where she never really wants him far from her sight), Marie never misses an opportunity to badmouth Debra, and doesn't even have a picture of Debra in her home...SERIES REGULAR (17)

[ROBERT]   A 40ish shlump in a police uniform, Robert is Ray's older brother, a police sergeant with a long set of problems: he still lives with his parents, he can't count past the number twelve without taking off his shoes, his girlfriend just left him for a convicted felon, and he compulsively touches his food to his chin before he eats. Maybe not the greatest role model on earth for his niece and nephews, Robert usually hangs out with his parents, and accompanies them when they show up at Ray's house uninvited and unexpected, but is much less outgoing than his parents. Robert has feelings of envy for his brother, and seems irked that Ray is able to make ends meet without getting shot at...SERIES REGULAR (24) *[Copyright 1996, BREAKDOWN SERVICES, LTD.]*

[LEO]   Ray's next door neighbor and best friend, Leo, is in his mid to late 30s and overweight. A married man with kids, Leo loves his

pizza, and likes to go with Ray and hang out at Nemo's, the neighborhood pizza joint. Deeply attracted to Nemo's grand-niece Angelina, Leo knows better than to even think of ever acting on his little infatuation, but that doesn't stop him from going by every night to drink in Angelina's bored waitress-y beauty. Expert at manipulating Ray into accompanying him on his excursions, Leo also mocks Ray for being caught as the middleman between his parents and his wife...SERIES REGULAR (15) *[Copyright 1996, BREAKDOWN SERVICES, LTD.]*

[ALLY]   The 5 year old daughter of Debra and Ray, Ally is a sweet little girl who likes to put peas in her eyes, and drives her mother crazy when she does. Energetic and rambunctious, Ally has learned just enough about human society to get her mother in trouble—like when she starts asking awkwardly pointed questions of fat people. But Ally doesn't know quite enough to stop her from breaking things, and her weary parents have keep a constant eye on her...SERIES REGULAR (1) *[Copyright 1996, BREAKDOWN SERVICES, LTD.]*

[GREGORY]   [MATTHEW]   Both one year old, Gregory and Matthew are the **TWIN SONS** of Ray and Debra. Still at a relatively pre-verbal stage, they are able to say "mo," scarf down Froot Loops, and knock the milk on the floor. They are a pair of perfectly normal children who are just energetic enough to drive their overburdened parents crazy...SERIES REGULAR (1) **PLEASE SUBMIT TWINS, TRIPLETS, AND QUINTS**

* *

[NEMO]   The owner and head chef of Nemo's Pizza, Nemo is an ancient Italian man who believes in complaining directly to Ray about the competence of the Knicks, apparently believing that sportswriter Ray can pass the word along. His pizza joint is the main hang-out for Leo and Ray...1 line, 1 scene (21) **THIS ROLE COULD POSSIBLY RECUR**

[ANGELINA]   A young, beautiful 20ish waitress, Angelina is Nemo's grand-niece, and the object of Leo's silent devotion. Completely bored at work, Angelina takes no notice of Leo's adoration as she takes his order…2 lines, 1 scene (22) **THIS ROLE COULD POSSIBLY RECUR**

STORYLINE: Ray is a sportswriter who is happily married to Debra, with three children: 5 year old ALLY and the 1 year old twins, GREGORY and MATTHEW. There's just one source of chaos in his life: his family, which doesn't quite grasp the concept of boundaries, and believes that Ray's home, children, and even his answering machine, are all put on this earth for them to enjoy…

DELIEVERED IN LA Thursday, August 1, 1996:
Start Date: 8/7/96

[NEMO]   The owner and head chef of Nemo's Pizza, Nemo believes in complaining to sportswriter Ray about the competence of the Jets. In contrast to his restaurant—which takes on a lovely, romantic ambience in the evening—Nemo still sports a filthy apron and is seen carrying some wet dough as he walks through the dining area…1 line, 1 scene (3) **THIS SMALL ROLE COULD POSSIBLY RECUR.**
[Copyright 1996, BREAKDOWN SERVICES, LTD.]

Will Power, Grace under Pressure

Will & Grace

The holiday season of 1997 was not going so merrily for casting director Tracy Lilienfield. She'd been charged with finding the four leads for a new sitcom by David Kohan and Max Mutchnick, whom she met when they worked as writers on the saucy HBO sitcom *Dream On*, and later on the short-lived NBC series *Boston Common*.

And she had found the ideal actor for the male lead: a suave, dark-haired Canadian with just the right comic timing and sexual energy to play an urbane gay lawyer in Manhattan.

His name was Eric McCormack. And he had passed on the role.

"Great 'Will' Hunting," was the heading for the Breakdown that went out to agents and managers on Dec. 19, 1997. "Desperately seeking the Will I've overlooked. Please submit the ONE actor who is perfect for this role but you couldn't get him an audition... Actors must be available for auditions Dec. 22 & 23... Your submission is your opportunity. We can be naughty or nice depending on your submission. Ho! Ho! Ho!"

Sitting in her corner office on the CBS/Radford lot in Studio City, where she's preparing for the seventh season of the NBC hit

Will & Grace, Lilienfield laughs as she looks back at this naked plea for a holiday surprise.

"I knew this would come back to haunt me," she says. "It's like I was losing my mind. I thought, Is this funny? Is it stupid? 'Ho! Ho! Ho!'

"I just thought this was a way, if I've overlooked someone, or if people have been trying to tell me for ten years they've got a fabulous guy and I'm not listening," to give them a shot, she explains. She even jokes that this wide-net "Will" hunt was "like a reality thing before its day—a contest."

We all know how the story turned out—McCormack was eventually won over—but did this last-minute pitch for alternate Wills yield any serious contenders?

"We tested some people, but we really were trying to get over [losing] Eric," she confesses. "We weren't ready to move on."

She had more than an emotional stake in to finding the right Will: The pilot was "cast contingent" at the time, meaning that it wouldn't shoot a frame unless the perfect leads were found—and thus wouldn't turn into a full-time casting gig for Lilienfield. (See the chapter on *Alias*.)

Lilienfield passed the holidays in doubt about the show's future, and not only because of uncertainty about the part of Will. The Grace she and the producers had fixed on, Debra Messing, was proving a tough sell, too. She was already on a series, *Prey*, and though that show's ratings were poor and the buzz was that it would be cancelled, Messing—who'd previously headlined the sitcom *Ned & Stacy*—wasn't especially eager to sign on for another series.

"She was tired, and she wasn't sure...that [*Prey*] would be cancelled. She was weighing very carefully what to do next. That wasn't easy either."

As if to prove that not every casting director can take full credit for every casting coup, Lilienfield reiterates a bit of TV lore.

"There's quite a famous story—that Max and David took tequila and showed up at her doorstep, and they drank all night and laughed and talked, and by the morning she was Grace."

To hear Lilienfield tell it, though, Messing already *was* Grace, described in the Breakdown as an "adorable, neurotic, happening

New York chick." She just needed Kohan and Mutchnick to come along and let her in on the secret.

"The way Debra *walked* was what they imagined," Lilienfield says, marveling at how perfectly all the show's cast members fit the parts as the writers conceived them. "I mean, everything about the way those actors are, and their kind of funny, is exactly what Max and David wanted them to be."

With one possible exception, actually: Megan Mullally's haughty, helium-voiced Karen, Grace's so-called assistant, whose purse is a traveling pharmacy and whose blood-alcohol level is seldom road-ready.

"Karen was the least well-defined character in the pilot," Lilienfield recalls. Indeed, the only mention of her in the Breakdown for the two leads is as Grace's "upscale assistant who leaves her to answer the phone." This meant that Mullally also had to be wooed to consider taking the part.

"Megan wasn't all that interested, because there wasn't much to play, especially compared to the other [parts]. But she was so fantastic and so funny and brought something special. She was different than most of the people we were looking at. And she was *absolutely* the only one we wanted at that point, by far."

The competition for talent that makes every pilot season a scramble made Lilienfield's job even harder—especially one fateful day, when Mullally was in contention for another network show.

"I remember she was testing for something else, and I was sure she was gonna get it—it might have been [for] Foxworthy," Lilienfield says. "So I said to [director James Burrows], 'Who do you think?' And he said, 'Megan Mullally.' And I said, 'Look, don't get your heart set, because she's testing for something else today. I'm sure she'll get it.' I mean, I can't imagine anyone not hiring her. 'So who's your second choice?' 'Megan Mullally.' I said, 'Jimmy, I'm not so sure I can deliver her. You better think if you like any of these other ones,' and he said, 'No, Megan Mullally.'

"And then of course I was on pins and needles all day, I called the casting director 100 times, and I found out [Megan] didn't get it. Oh my God, she didn't get it!

"And then she still didn't want to come in," Lilienfield recalls. "It was down to the morning of the test, and she was the only we were testing—she didn't know that. I called her at home and begged and cajoled. I think she really had no intention of testing. But she did, thank goodness."

The feeling was mutual, as Lilienfield remembers it: "After the test—she came in, she got it, they loved her—I walked out and I said to her, 'Did I ruin your life? 'Cause you got it.'" And she said, 'No, no.' By that time she said she was excited."

Karen still didn't figure heavily in the pilot, nor had Mullally or the writers zeroed in on the character as we know it today. She didn't use that signature high-pitched voice, for one thing (which isn't Mullally's normal speaking voice). But something happened over the summer of 1998, after the show was picked up and ready to go to air.

"She went away for the summer and came back, and Karen was way more fully formed by the time we started the series," Lilienfield recalls. "She came back and we were like, 'Whoa, she found Karen!'"

Finally, there was perhaps *Will & Grace*'s signature role, its Fonz, its Urkel, its Barney Fife—i.e., the purportedly supporting role which comes to define a series' everlasting place in the small-screen pantheon. I'm speaking, of course, of Jack, the ultra-effeminate gay imp who has swished his way into the living rooms of America with his irresistibly pert comic timing and an unashamedly, boyishly libidinous gleam in his eye.

There is another piece of TV lore behind Sean Hayes' nabbing the role. Reportedly, as he left the audition room, he snapped his head around toward the producers and sassily demanded: "Are you looking at my ass?"

But Hayes needed persuading, too, as it turned out. A gay-themed independent film in which he starred, *Billy's Hollywood Screen Kiss*, was wowing audiences at the Sundance Film Festival that February, and the journeyman actor (remember his performance in that Doritos commercial as a guy struck dumb by the sight of Ali Landry?) was finally in a position to be choosy.

"That [film] was huge, and that was happening as we were casting this," Lilienfield recalls. "He was at Sundance and he was sort of the toast of the town, and not so wanting to come back here."

OUT AND ABOUT

Now that many urban-set sitcoms feature a gay character or two, it's almost hard to recall the "bad old days" when such characters were the exclusive province of late-night comedies (*Soap*) or the occasional Movie of the Week (*An Early Frost*).

Ellen DeGeneres' sitcom famously busted open the TV closet, and it may be that she was ahead of her time; the show survived only one full season after she came out, both on- and off-screen. Or it may simply have been that her modestly funny, *Seinfeld*-esque show wasn't the ideal vehicle to introduce a gay milieu to mainstream audiences. Nor, arguably, is DeGeneres particularly "gay" in her comic sensibility; she's as middle-of-the-road all-American as Bob Newhart, and while it makes a powerful statement that such a TV-friendly comic also happens to be gay, that's a political point without a punchline.

What *Will & Grace* proved from the start was that unabashed, undisguised urban gay humor could find an audience in the mainstream, just as other distinct styles of comedy fostered in minority subcultures—African-American, Jewish, Southern white working-class—have been embraced by Middle America.

Still, when the casting Breakdown went out, there were no precedents for a gay sitcom, or an openly gay network sitcom lead. The description of Will calls him "an accessibly handsome, masculine, witty and devilishly charming gay man." There are few leading actors in Hollywood who would object to the first four adjectives being applied to them—but did the character's sexuality give any actors cold feet?

"I would just say that *maybe* a few people passed because of that," Lilienfield recalls. "A few people flat-out said so; [with] a few people, I sort of read it between the lines. But it was barely anything to have to contend with it."

Lilienfield says she read "lots and lots of straight actors," including McCormack.

McCormack, in fact, is someone Lilienfield had in mind from the start.

"I wanted him in the first day of auditions, but he was in Canada, because he was mostly still living in Canada," Lilienfield says. "I think he came in on the second day."

After winning the part and having it offered, though, McCormack passed, leading to Lilienfield's holiday hunt.

"Sure, we tested people," she said. "We didn't think we had Eric, so we tried. But we couldn't get a consensus [on anyone else], thank God."

Indeed, in retrospect, it's especially fortunate that they didn't, since the pressures of pilot season can often force a casting director's hand.

"When you're in the midst of it, you're not expecting perfection, you're expecting, 'Hmm, that could work,'" Lilienfield says. "There were people who maybe could have worked, but [the show] never would have become what it is."

After playing hard to get, McCormack "came back on his own." When he tested with Messing, the match was sealed.

"We tested Eric and Debra together at [James Burrows'] house," Lilienfield recalls. "It was a Saturday thing, I forget why—some scheduling problem. But it turned out to be fantastic, of course; it was like a party, and everyone was in their jeans, not their executive clothing, in Jimmy's beautiful family room, on his beautiful property, with his Wolfgang Puck-catered brunch."

She's quick to amend one aspect of her recollection: "It actually wasn't a test. We called it a 'chemistry read,' but it turned out to be all that was necessary."

Lilienfield, who since cast (and recast) *Good Morning, Miami* for Kohan and Mutchnick, clearly holds *Will & Grace* in a special esteem. It's one of those shows whose snug fit of actors to roles has a kind of kismet about it.

"It really is one of those miracle ones where it's seamless—you couldn't even begin to remember or imagine it being different," Lilienfield says. "The synergy was perfect always—between the characters, the actors, and Max and David."

Indeed, it's clear that the challenges of casting *Will & Grace* were centered on persuading those right actors to come on board, not finding them in the first place. As Lilienfield explains, time and talent were on her side.

"It was really good material, so everybody in town was interested in it," Lilienfield recalls. "It wasn't like I couldn't get somebody to come in. And we were early, and so it wasn't like people were not available. We took a good long time, and we did not finish till late."

And, whatever last-minute tap-dancing she had to do when the ideal "fab four" were proving elusive, she says there was never a question of who the producers wanted—just a question of how to get them.

"It wasn't like, I'm taking three [favorites], and whoever gets it, gets it. It was absolutely, *specifically*, these four people who were all we wanted."

(File: 1125p01-dg) L
NBC ENTERTAINMENT
"WILL AND GRACE"
1/2 HOUR PILOT/NBC

DELIVERED IN NY Tue., Nov. 25, 1997
Producers: David Kohan/ Max Mutchnick
Writers: David Kohan/ Max Mutchnick
LA Casting Director: TBA
NY Casting Director: Steven O'Neill
Location: LA
Start Date: TBA

WRITTEN SUBMISSIONS ONLY TO: STEVEN O'NEILL

[WILL HERMAN]   In his early 30s, he's an accessibly handsome, masculine, witty, and devilishly charming gay man. A corporate lawyer with his own small firm, Will's straight law partner, Andy, is the legal eagle, while Will professes to be the king of negotiations and schmoozers. Having recently broken up with his long-time lover, Will has bounced back quite nicely, due in part, no doubt, to his very warm and fuzzy relationship with Grace, his loveable soulmate. Whether sharing the experience of watching *ER* while on the phone together, or playing "$25,000 Pyramid," they make the perfect couple—except she's straight and he's gay. Grace always comes first in Will's life and that tends to make their "strange" relationship, dating back to their college days, a bit confusing for his other pals. Not one to be shy about giving his brutally honest opinion, Will holds back when Grace asks his advice on marrying her boyfriend. He later tests their closeness by refusing to give his blessing…LEAD (*Copyright 2003, BREAKDOWN SERVICES, LTD.*) **SUBMIT ALL ETHNICITIES**

[GRACE ADLER]   She's 30, an adorable, neurotic, happening New York chick who owns an interior design company. Grace's friendship with Will is very special, very close, and very platonic—she's straight, he's gay. Their intimate knowledge of one another is a sharp contrast to what she has with Danny, her live-in boyfriend, who scarcely knows

her. Grace has trouble managing her life. She has an upscale assistant who leaves her to answer the phone and a boyfriend who doesn't appreciate her. But she has lucked out in her relationship with Will, a playmate and confidante extraordinaire. When Grace's rocky relationship with Danny hits a few bumps, she runs to Will for comfort and a temporary place to stay. And when Danny finally proposes, she asks Will to give her his sincere blessing, but gets something else entirely…LEAD *(Copyright 2003, BREAKDOWN SERVICES, LTD.)*
SUBMIT ALL ETHNICITIES

STORYLINE: Will's good intentions go awry when his friend Jack thinks he's a welcomed houseguest, but a sudden crisis has Will's best friend, Grace, moving in instead…

(File: 1125p02-cb) L
(Original File: 1125p01-dg) N
NBC ENTERTAINMENT
"WILL AND GRACE"
1/2 HOUR PILOT/NBC

DELIVERED IN LA Wed, Nov. 26, 1997
Producers: David Kohan/ Max Mutchnick
Writers: David Kohan/ Max Mutchnick
LA Casting Director: Tracy Lilienfield
Location: LA
Start Date: TBA

WRITTEN SUBMISSIONS ONLY TO: TRACY LILIENFIELD

[WILL HERMAN]   27-32, he's an accessibly handsome, masculine, witty, and devilishly charming gay man. A corporate lawyer with his own small firm, Will's straight law partner, Andy, is the legal eagle, while Will professes to be the king of negotiations and schmoozers. Having recently broken up with his long-time lover, Will has bounced back quite nicely, due in part, no doubt, to his very warm and fuzzy relationship with Grace, his loveable soulmate. Whether sharing the experience of watching *ER* while on the phone together, or playing "$25,000 Pyramid," they make the perfect couple—except she's straight and he's gay. Grace always comes first in Will's life and that tends to make their "strange" relationship, dating back to their college days, a bit confusing for his other pals. Not one to be shy about giving his brutally honest opinion, Will holds back when Grace asks his advice on marrying her boyfriend. He later tests their closeness by refusing to give his blessing…LEAD *(Copyright 2003, BREAKDOWN SERVICES, LTD.)*

[GRACE ADLER]   She's 27-32, an adorable, neurotic, happening New York chick who owns an interior design company. Grace's friendship with Will is very special, very close, and very platonic— she's straight, he's gay. Their intimate knowledge of one another is a sharp contrast to what she has with Danny, her live-in boyfriend, who scarcely knows her. Grace has trouble managing her life. She has an upscale assistant who leaves her to answer the phone and a

boyfriend who doesn't appreciate her. But she has lucked out in her relationship with Will, a playmate and confidante extraordinaire. When Grace's rocky relationship with Danny hits a few bumps, she runs to Will for comfort and a temporary place to stay. And when Danny finally proposes, she asks Will to give her his sincere blessing, but gets something else entirely…LEAD *(Copyright 2003, BREAKDOWN SERVICES, LTD.)*

STORYLINE: Will's good intentions go awry when his friend Jack thinks he's a welcomed houseguest, but a sudden crisis has his best friend, Grace, moving in instead…

BREAKDOWN SERVICES, LTD. | Los Angeles (310) 276-9166 | New York (212) 869-2003 | Vancouver (604) 943-7100 | London (01) 459-2781 | The information contained in this document is the exclusive property of Breakdown Services, Ltd. Any unauthorized reproduction, duplication, copying or use of the information contained herein, without prior written consent of Breakdown Services, Ltd., is strictly prohibited.

BREAKDOWN SERVICES, LTD.
www.breakdownservices.com   The Link: www.submitlink.com

(File: 1218p03-lj) L
(Prev.: 1125p02})
Original File: 1125p01-dg) N
NBC ENTERTAINMENT
"WILL AND GRACE"
1/2 HOUR PILOT/NBC

DEL'D IN LA Fri., Dec. 19, 1997, Vol. 1997 #1219
Producers: David Kohan/ Max Mutchnick
Writers: David Kohan/ Max Mutchnick
LA Casting Director: Tracy Lilienfield
Casting Associate: Paris Morra
Location: LA
Start Date: TBA

WRITTEN SUBMISSIONS ONLY TO: TRACY LILIENFIELD

A previous breakdown was released on Nov. 26.

Sides will be available through _Sides Express_

GREAT "WILL" HUNTING:

Desperately seeking the Will I've overlooked. Please submit the **_ONE_** actor who is perfect for this role but you couldn't get him to the audition. All submissions containing your **_ONE_** favorite perfect suggestion will be seriously considered. Actors must be available for auditions December 22nd and 23rd. No phone calls, please. Your submission is your opportunity. We can be naughty or nice depending on your submission. Ho! Ho! Ho!

[WILL HERMAN]   **Caucasian 27-34,** he's an accessibly handsome, masculine, witty, and devilishly charming gay man. A corporate lawyer with his own small firm, Will's straight law partner, Andy, is the legal eagle, while Will professes to be the king of negotiations and schmoozers. Having recently broken up with his long-time lover, Will has bounced back quite nicely, due in part, no doubt, to his very warm and fuzzy relationship with Grace, his loveable soulmate. Whether sharing the experience of watching *ER* while on the phone together, or playing "$25,000 Pyramid," they make the perfect couple—except she's straight and he's gay. Grace always comes first

in Will's life and that tends to make their "strange" relationship, dating back to their college days, a bit confusing for his other pals. Not one to be shy about giving his brutally honest opinion, Will holds back when Grace asks his advice on marrying her boyfriend. He later tests their closeness by refusing to give his blessing...LEAD

STORYLINE: Will's good intentions go awry when his friend Jack thinks he's a welcomed houseguest, but a sudden crisis has his best friend, Grace, moving in instead...

(Copyright 2003, BREAKDOWN SERVICES, LTD.)

(File 0130p10-lk) L
(P. 0129p03, O. 1125p01)
NBC ENTERTAINMENT
"WILL AND GRACE"
1/2 HOUR PILOT/ NBC

DEL'D IN LA Mon., Feb. 2, 1998, Vol. 1998, #0202
Producers: David Kohan/ Max Mutchnick
Director: James Burrows
Writers: David Kohan/ Max Mutchnick
LA Casting Director: Tracy Lilienfield
Casting Associate: Paris Morra
Location: L.A.
Start Date: March 12

WRITTEN SUBMISSIONS ONLY TO: TRACY LILIENFIELD

Previous breakdowns have been released.

Sides will be available through Sides Express

WILL: CAST (ERIC McCORMACK)

[GRACE ADLER] She's 27-32, an adorable, neurotic, happening New York chick who owns an interior design company. Grace's friendship with Will is very special, very close, and very platonic— she's straight, he's gay. Their intimate knowledge of one another is a sharp contrast to what she has with Danny, her live-in boyfriend, who scarcely knows her. Grace has trouble managing her life. She has an upscale assistant who leaves her to answer the phone and a boyfriend who doesn't appreciate her. But she has lucked out in her relationship with Will, a playmate and confidante extraordinaire. When Grace's rocky relationship with Danny hits a few bumps, she runs to Will for comfort and a temporary place to stay. And when Danny finally proposes, she asks Will to give her his sincere blessing, but gets something else entirely...SERIES REGULAR *(Copyright 2004, BREAKDOWN SERVICES, LTD.)*

[JACK MACFARLAND] 28-33. He's Will's long time buddy, a really loyal, really grating, and really gay man with a ferret-like energy and

BREAKDOWN SERVICES, LTD. Los Angeles   New York   Vancouver   London
BREAKDOWN SERVICES; LTD: (310) 276-9166 (212) 869-2003 (604) 943-7100 (01) 459-2781
BREAKDOWN SERVICES; LTD:
BREAKDOWN SERVICES; LTD:
BREAKDOWN SERVICES, LTD.
www.breakdownservices.com   The Link: www.submitlink.com

a trust fund. He lives with his mother and his pet macaw, Guapo, and likes to sing Steve and Eydie songs while playing poker with the boys. At present, Jack is having problems with mom and asks Will if he can move in for awhile. When he arrives—with his matching Louis Vuitton luggage and caged Guapo—he finds Grace has taken his spot and the melodrama begins. Jack just can't get over playing second fiddle to Grace and after a couple more attempts to move in, he resigns to the fact that Grace is there to stay...SERIES REGULAR (6)

[ANDY FELNER] 28-36. He is Will's new legal eagle corporate law partner, a straight and narrow-minded guy, though his personal ads say otherwise. Andy is terribly insecure and doubts his value to Will. After he turns off a client with his legalese, he laments that he should never be left alone with clients, better he should "be in some little law hut drafting agreements." Although he tries to one-up Will's wickedness, he just doesn't have it in him. He's better suited for lending a supportive ear now and then...SERIES REGULAR (6) PLEASE SUBMIT ALL ETHNICITIES, EXCEPT CAUCASIAN.

[KAREN WALKER] 29, she's Grace's fabulously wealthy, flamboyant assistant whose—Diva attitude could easily get her mistaken for the CEO. Karen dons a mink and sunglasses as she makes her routinely late entrance to the office and ignores Will's routine demands that Grace fire her. She would rather rattle off advice to Grace on "closing the deal" in her relationship with Danny than answer phones. She's got it made working "for" Grace and she knows it—if only Will weren't around...SERIES REGULAR (23)

STORYLINE: Will's good intentions go awry when his friend Jack MacFarland thinks he's a welcome houseguest, but a sudden crisis has Will's best friend, Grace, moving in instead...
(Copyright 2004, BREAKDOWN SERVICES, LTD., All Rights Reserved)

One Ring to Rule, Several Ways to Cast

The Lord of the Rings

Critics and fans have long searched for real-life geopolitical parallels to J.R.R. Tolkien's *The Lord of the Rings* trilogy (Was Mordor a stand-in for the Third Reich? Stalin's Soviet Union?). And certainly the fortuitous timing of Peter Jackson's definitive three-part film adaptation, released coincidentally over three years in the midst of international headlines highlighting terrorism and war, inspired fresh comparisons between Middle Earth's fictional battles and our current actual ones.

But who knew that the casting of Jackson's films would be a test of American national character?

"In my first meeting with Peter, he said, 'I'm just going to have you work on the eight roles that we're looking to be possibly American,'" recalls Los Angeles-based casting director Victoria Burrows. Indeed, she says, Jackson expected that he would find his four hobbits in London, where casting directors John and Ros Hubbard were stationed; or in New Zealand, where his longtime casting director Liz Mullane was on the lookout; or even in Australia, where casting director Ann Robinson had set up shop.

Burrows, and partner Scot Boland, would hear none of it.

"I said, 'Look, if Brits can speak with American accents, we Americans can speak with British accents,'" she recalls. "I said, 'Let [us] run with all eighteen roles; I won't charge you any more.' He was really hesitant; he did not believe that we would find Frodo and the hobbits." In short, Burrows says, "No one figured the U.S. would deliver."

It was not for lack of interest from American actors and their representatives, who flocked to Burrows' and Boland's office to read the scripts—the only place they could see them, in fact. In a uniquely top-secret arrangement, the casting directors had only one copy of the script for each of the three films, which could not be copied or be taken outside their office.

"Actors and agents had to come in and read it in the office," Burrows says. Auditioning actors couldn't even take a copy of their "sides"—script excerpts for the scenes they'd be reading—and go outside the audition room to prepare.

"They could not take it with them to go," says Burrows. "So actors had to come in an hour early, or a half hour—whatever they felt their prep time was—and do it in the room, and then leave the material with us."

Actors who were happy to oblige included Ryan Philippe and Jake Gyllenhaal, both interested in the part of Frodo; Vin Diesel, who so passionately craved the heroic role of Aragorn that he put himself on tape in character, and wouldn't consider other roles Burrows suggested, such as the warrior Faramir; Ethan Hawke, who was in talks to play Faramir, and his wife, Uma Thurman, considered for the supporting role of Eowyn; Jon Voight, who met with director Jackson about the roles of Gandalf and Theoden, and Martin Landau, who discussed the part of the evil wizard Saruman.

Actors were so eager to get a whack at the material that some even showed up in Middle Earth costumes—usually a huge audition no-no, but in this case a practice Burrows and Boland welcomed. Recounts Boland, "We basically had every—I don't know what the word is, but if you call *Trek* fans Trekkies, you had every 'hobbit fan' come out of the woodwork for this. You weren't laughing at it so much as you were impressed that they'd committed so much to really trying to serve the picture."

Not only did she make allowances for creative wardrobe, Burrows says she gladly worked with actors to suspend disbelief in the audition room.

"A lot of cold readings, when an actor comes in and reads, they're sitting in chairs or walking around a bit," Burrows explains. Not in this case, she recounts: "So many of [the actors] had to get on the ground and act the roles. It was very different from normal film acting. So I got on the floor with them and read with them, acting that out. They had to create more of that in the audition, because of the period piece that it was. We all got much more involved, not only emotionally but in acting out the scenes, and the actors really put their hearts and souls into it."

In the midst of this high-profile fan convention, it was a call from Elijah Wood's agent that turned things around for *The Lord of the Rings*' underdog U.S. outpost.

"The agent asked, 'Elijah so loves this material—would you mind if he put something on tape and sent it to you?' And we said, 'With what he's doing and what he thinks, absolutely; we look forward to seeing what it looks like.'" Burrows says she still has a copy of this now-legendary tape, in which Wood had himself filmed as Frodo in a Shire-like setting. Indeed, it was this tape more than Burrows' word that finally convinced Jackson.

"When I called him up and said, 'We found Frodo,' he was like, 'Ha ha, right,'" Burrows recalls. "I said, 'Wait, I'm going to send you this tape.' After I sent it, Peter called and said, 'You're right. Don't tell Elijah—I want to get him in the room, I want to see him. But all said and done, I think we're going to go with him.'"

Burrows also campaigned for Sean Astin in the key role of Samwise, Frodo's loyal companion ("Sean worked very hard," Burrows says), and set up the deals with John-Rhys Davies, an English actor based in L.A., for the role of the crusty dwarf Gimli, and Miranda Otto, an Aussie actress whose manager happened to be in L.A. at the time, for the role of Eowyn.

But Burrows' and Boland's work wasn't done by the time the first day of shooting came around. There was yet one more emergency mission for the U.S. casting crew: Replacing Jackson's first choice for the lead role of Aragorn, a twenty-six-year-old British actor named Stuart Townsend, who was apparently proving too young-seeming in rehearsals. Townsend was fired the day before shooting began—and then the scramble for his replacement began.

"You never know the truth about these situations," says John Hubbard, the seasoned London casting director for the film, demurring on the question of why Townsend was canned. He does remember how the young actor got the part, though: "Stuart came in for another part—for Faramir, a young prince. And Peter said, 'I'd like him to read for Aragorn.' And I said, 'I thought Aragorn was like a sort of mature warrior, with enormous battle experience.' I recall Peter saying, 'Yes, but I have a young audience, and I don't want to make the mistake of casting too many older characters.' I said, 'Fine,' but I still wondered about that."

Burrows, too, attributes Townsend's mismatch primarily to age.

"That was Stuart's hardest thing—he was young," Burrows says. "And you needed this kind of manly man to come out."

One actor Burrows felt "innately had that in him" was forty-one-year-old Viggo Mortensen, an American, at the time respected in the business but well short of stardom. Indeed, Mortensen had been on Burrows' list from early on, but he wasn't available to meet with Jackson when the director breezed through Los Angeles for a mere three days of meetings with Burrows' top choices.

But now that Townsend was out of the picture, Mortensen's name came up again—and it was a nail-biting near-miss, Burrows recalls.

"I had felt strongly about Viggo for a long time, and his manager knew that," she says. The only problem: Not only had the elusive Mortensen been unavailable when Jackson visited L.A., he was incommunicado when Burrows and company tried to find him again. "He was where there were no phones, so his manager tracked him down. Then he read it, and then there were negotiations. His son was really instrumental in getting him to do this: 'It's OK, Dad—you're in *Lord of the Rings*!' His son was reading the books at the time."

The deal was done by the end of the film's first week of shooting. Mortensen was hustled onto a plane to New Zealand—but not before getting a teary sendoff the night before.

"We had really worked hard on it for a week, the deal, and keeping it quiet as the transition was being made," Burrows recalls. "We all cried at Paco's Tacos, cheering that we were putting him on the plane—the agent, the manager, Viggo, and I all had dinner to celebrate. We were so happy that it all worked."

For his part, Hubbard is philosophical about the Aragorn recasting.

"You know, we all make mistakes; directors make mistakes," Hubbard says. "I think something like this, where you're casting for three massive movies, a massively complex choreography of people, and on top of that you're thinking about special effects—the pressure on Peter must have been the most pressure any film director's ever gone through in the history of film. Trying to have an overview, trying to keep your eye on something, and just for a second the eye went off the ball."

ENGLISH SPOKEN HERE

Burrows' and Boland's casting coups in these key roles are all the more remarkable given that the majority of the film's actors are English—and rightly so, as Hubbard points out.

"Peter was very respectful to the fact that Tolkien was British," Hubbard says. "And also that the Middle Earth was by and large Warwickshire, which is where Tolkien lived as a child outside Birmingham, and later lived in Birmingham city. So there was very much a feeling that Peter wanted to be faithful to that, and to the fact that the characters were quite English—I don't even say British, they were *English*. I don't think it was patronizing; I don't think it was like, you know, sometimes Americans come to Britain, and the character's an English boy, and they see five boys in London, and then they go back and cast it in America.

"I think [Peter] was just being very sensitive—to the family, to the fact that it was very much an English classic. And the fact that the book, though it's in a strange land, had a sort of very specific, unique British medieval feel about it, especially the opening scenes in the Shire, and the [Bilbo Baggins] character."

So how did his London office receive the notion of American hobbits? Like Burrows and Boland, Hubbard was sold by Elijah Wood's irresistible tape.

"Peter and myself and Fran [Walsh] sat down and watched it, and it was just fantastic," Hubbard says. And perhaps most important: "His accent was brilliant."

The filmmakers' respect for the material's national origin aside, Hubbard felt no proprietary claim on the roles.

"At the end of the day, it was the best actor," he says. "It was like, 'I'm not going to say anybody has to be English, or has to be this, has to be that.' The whole thing has an English flavor about it, and in the end there's mostly British actors."

Interestingly enough, while British actors were at least as keen as their American counterparts to be part of a beloved book, they didn't come in costume to auditions or crawl on the floor.

"That's the different cultures—you never, *ever* turn up in wardrobe to a British casting, where in America, it's quite common," Hubbard says. He couldn't resist relating a colorful example of this cultural divide: "There was a wonderful story about an English director in Hollywood, casting sort of a cricket commercial. The brief was, he wanted two batsmen. And he turns up to the casting and there's a room full of people wearing masks and capes— they thought it was *Batman*."

In costume or not, many British actors' passion for the material did run high, and Hubbard, like Burrows, found himself uncharacteristically indulgent.

"We certainly saw a lot of actors who *really* wanted to be in the film; the agents were very, very clear, 'Please, John, he has to be seen for this.' And for me, I wasn't as judgmental as I normally am about actors. Anybody who rings about any film I will see; I may not let them meet the director if I don't know them, but, you know, I'll read with you and we'll talk about it. So we saw a lot of actors who just were massive fans and *had* to be in the film."

Passion wouldn't cut it, though, for the physical requirements of some roles, either in the U.K. or the U.S.

"Anyone who was being considered for a hobbit couldn't be over 5'9"," recalls Scot Boland. They weren't messing around with that prerequisite, says Burrows: "Jake Gyllenhaal flew himself in, but when he walked in the door, we had measuring tape, and he was definitely 5'10", if not 5'10" and a quarter."

In at least one case, though, height didn't preclude a qualified actor from consideration.

"We were responsible for bringing to the table John Rhys-Davies, who played [the dwarf] Gimli," says Burrows. "Now, that man is six feet tall, but they were able to work it to where he obviously looked tiny."

CASTING JAMBOREE

While Townsend was the only actor who was actually replaced, a look back at the casting directors' lists provides a fascinating window onto some alternative *Lord of the Rings* casts.

Hubbard lays out his three-ring binder on a conference room table in his London office.

"*Jamboree*, Saturday, November 14, 1998, eight pages of ideas," he reads off the page. For those who are wondering: *Jamboree* was the code name for *The Lord of the Rings* projects—a cloak-and-dagger practice which bemuses Hubbard. "I don't ever really understand these things, because in Hollywood, everybody knows exactly what's going on. We have a film with Columbia that [my wife] Ros and I are both producing; it started November 1, in New York. The agents in America ring me up and go, 'I hear John Cusack really likes your script, and I hear Columbia are after him.' It's like, Crikey, I just spoke to them last night!"

Back to his list, which Hubbard checks to jog his memory ("This is about fifty projects back now"). He re-reads his introductory disclaimer for Jackson and Walsh: "We've thrown everybody into the mix. Obviously time and money will militate against the involvement of some of the best known names. Let me know if you need credits. I've added others off the ICM list that we think are right... Would it be a good idea to send a pack of pictures and CDs of the people you do not know, or would you prefer to get out videos?"

He glances across the list and finds a few intriguing notes: "'Eowyn, Kate Winslet'... 'Will Christopher Lee read?' Paul Scofield is there."

Was Scofield considered for Gandalf, we wonder?

"For Saruman," says Hubbard, referring to Gandalf's nemesis, a part that went to horror film icon Christopher Lee. Lee won the role with two inarguable bona fides: "When Christopher Lee came in, he said, 'I read the books up to three times every year, and have done for years and years and years.' And I think he's probably the only actor we met in the casting anywhere in the world who'd actually *met* Tolkien—met him in a pub in Oxford. He told Peter the story."

Besides, recalls Hubbard with a laugh, "Gene Diamond, [Lee's] agent, said, 'How will I handle him, John? He'll be so upset that he wasn't seen.' And it was clear that he was perfect for that part."

Other intriguing names that popped up were Mark Addy (*The Full Monty*, *Still Standing*) for Samwise Gamgee; Tim Roth and Daniel Craig (*Sylvia*) for Boromir; Elizabeth Hurley for Arwen, the elfin princess played in the films by Liv Tyler (Burrows recalls that Ashley Judd and Milla Jovovich were among those also considered for Arwen), and, for Gandalf, an unlikely roster of names: Terence Stamp (*The Limey*, *The Hit*), Tom Baker (*Dr. Who*), Patrick Stewart, Christopher Plummer, John Hurt—even David Bowie!

"There's somebody who obviously is a big fan of the books," is all Hubbard would say about that last name.

Given that Gandalf gridlock, Hubbard doesn't recall exactly how Sir Ian McKellen was singled out from the pack for the role—only that the meeting to discuss the part took place with Jackson at McKellen's house. Burrows says McKellen was just an obvious choice: "He asked me, 'Are you responsible?' I said, 'We're all responsible—you're so wonderful, you're going to be on everyone's list.'"

Hubbard scoffs slightly at the first choice listed for Aragorn: the mercurial Daniel Day Lewis, who has mostly given up acting to work as a cobbler in Florence, Italy—and not, it seems, as research for a role.

"You know, anybody who comes in here and says, 'I've written for Daniel Day Lewis,' I say, 'Well, it's never gonna happen, is it?' He's not in our business, you know? He came out for Scorsese, and he'll come out for Jim Sheridan, possibly. Anybody else, no."

Another Englishman on Hubbard's original list gave Burrows and Boland another chance to score one for the Americans: Richard

O'Brien, the star and creator of the pop culture phenomenon *The Rocky Horror Show* (the stage predecessor to the cult film), was lined up to play the small but memorable part of Wormtongue, a pale, hissing quisling who appears in the second film, *The Two Towers*.

"He came in, he was very interested in doing it," Hubbard says. "And then he rang me, saying, 'I don't know, John, what do you think?' And I said, 'I don't know. I mean, I love Peter, his work is fantastic, he's one of the true, rare, visionary directors alive that we have; there's only about five in the world.' He said, 'Oh, I don't want to go to New Zealand for three weeks.' And he turned it down. I don't know whether he cares now or not."

The part eventually went to the American actor Brad Dourif. Another American actor with a similar story—but for a much bigger part—ought to be kicking himself now, according to Burrows.

"For [the hobbit] Meridoc, I got Breckin Meyer as the first offer," Burrows says. Meyer is probably best known to audiences as the good-natured stoner from the film *Clueless*. "Breckin passed because he felt he wasn't going to get enough screen time, and not enough vacation tickets back and forth from New Zealand to Los Angeles. Which was, in my opinion, the worst mistake he's probably made in his career—and we still tease him about it. This film was one of those special ones where you get on board—especially with someone like Peter Jackson, who is such a visionary and who so embraces the cast and listens and hears, and fine-tunes it, always to the better."

Another young actor whose prominent role in *Lord of the Rings* has since catapulted his career almost didn't even get in the door.

"Daniel, my son, who is like the hot new casting director [in town], said, Would I meet Orlando [Bloom]?" Hubbard says. "Orlando is a friend of his; they're very good friends. And I said, 'No, I don't think he has the chops for this.' And he said, 'Well, Dad, would you see him for me?' And I said, 'Of course I would.' And Orlando starts reading, and I said, 'This is terrific—he's really good.' What I didn't know is that Dan, the night before, for an hour, had gone over the scenes, got Orlando's energy up, his confidence."

Probably the most unconventional bit of casting was for the part of Gollum—an emaciated little monster who was once a hobbit but whose crazed avarice, fueled by the ring, has shriveled him to a mere wisp of flesh and bone. No actor could have pulled off the look Jackson had in mind—elaborate computer animation would do the trick—but he nevertheless wanted an actor on-set, playing Gollum, for the other performers to react to, and to give the character its distinctively chilling voice. Apart from a brief introduction in the third film, *The Return of the King*, in which we flash back to Gollum's previous existence as the hobbit Smeagol, the actor playing Gollum would not be seen on-screen at all.

Hubbard has been casting long enough to expect one thing of every project: There will always be at least one role that seems impossible to fill. And he figured with Gollum, he'd found it.

"We've done 150 movies, and every movie has a character you go up to the wire on, because you can't for some reason crack it," Hubbard says. "Like *The Commitments*, for example, I didn't know it was going to be [the trumpet player] Joey the Lips. Johnny Murphy was seen in the very first week of casting. And [director Alan Parker] never told us that he had an actor who could do it. If he did, we would not have worked so hard trying to find an even better Joey who could play the trumpet: Van Morrison was met, Rory Gallagher, some of the great musicians. And in the end Alan said, 'OK, offer it to Johnny Murphy.' And it was like, 'What?'

"I thought Gollum was going to be the one on *Lord of the Rings*. I was thinking, How are we going to do Gollum? Because he's not there as an actor. But it was the easiest; it got cast so quickly. The first guy who came in was Andy Serkis. He just got into the shape and this hissing voice came out. He'd really prepared. Andy says he saw my jaw drop open, like, 'Where the fuck did that come from?'

"Later, on the phone, Peter said, 'How are we doing with Gollum?' And I said, 'Well, there's just one actor.' And he said, 'Oh, do people not want to do it?' I said, 'Just watch the tape.'" At the callback with Jackson, the choice was so clear that Jackson started to address Serkis as if he had the job: "Peter started talking about, 'When you come down to New Zealand...' And Andy outside the room is going, 'What's that mean, John? Does it mean I've got the part?' I said, 'Stop, Andy, I don't know. Stay cool, go away, forget about it.' And then very soon after Peter said, 'He's the one.'"

Near misses, negotiations, and Anglo-American competition aside, *The Lord of the Rings* boasts a cast for the ages. Perhaps because of the extensive and collaborative nature of the pre-production process, Burrows hesitates to take credit for all the film's inspired casting choices.

"It is teamwork. You're trying to serve the director's vision. Peter is good at expressing what he wants, so everything was really clear.

"It was fun looking for the cast—you saw everybody loving the material, loving the process. A couple of people got upset that they didn't move forward, but that happens in anything. I am just so lucky that I was involved with it; to me it's a piece of history—a modern-day classic."

NEW LINE CINEMA
"LORD OF THE RINGS"
THREE FULL LENGTH
FEATURE FILMS

DEL'D IN LA Mon., Jan. 11, 1999, Vol. 1999, #0111
Producers: Peter Jackson, Tim Sanders
Writers: Peter Jackson, Fran Walsh, Stephen Sinclair,
Philippa Boyens
USA Casting Directors: Victoria Burrows/Scot Boland
USA Casting Associate: Jenne Herbst
USA Casting Assistant: Sonja Lopez
UK Casting Director: Hubbard Casting
Australia Casting: Mullinars Casting Consultants
New Zealand Casting: Liz Mullane
Shoots: Sept. 1999–March 2001 (See below)
Location: New Zealand

WRITTEN SUBMISSIONS ONLY TO: VICTORIA BURROWS

NOTE: LORD OF THE RINGS comprises three full length feature films, for this purpose called Part One, Part Two, and Part Three. Part One shoots Sept. 19, 1999–Feb. 17, 2000. Part Two shoots May 21, 2000–Oct. 12, 2000. Part Three shoots Oct. 29, 2000–March 22, 2001.

LORD OF THE RINGS is set in a mythical world populated by several different races or types of "people:" Hobbits (FRODO, SAM, MERRY, PIPPIN, BILBO), Elves (ELROND, ARWEN, LEGOLAS), Dwarves (GIMLI), and Humans (ARAGORN, GANDALF, BOROMIR, DENETHOR, THEODEN, SANUMAN, FARAMIR, EOMYN).

For the **HOBBITS** it is our intention to cast actors of a normal height and use computer graphics to make them appear smaller. This will require the actors to shoot some of their scenes against blue screen, often reacting to a piece of tape, rather than other actors. The four main Hobbits are young, fit, and with the possible exception of Sam, lean. It is likely the most suitable hobbit actor will be around 5 ft. 6 inches. They are also of a similar age, with Frodo and Sam being obviously older than Merry and Pippin. We will probably use

prosthetics to a limited degree—ears, and maybe noses. They will wear prosthetic feet, a little larger than normal. **ACCENT: BRITISH**.

For the **HUMANS** the men of Middle-Earth are essentially no different to us. There are no special notes regarding human characters, other than that most will HAVE TO RIDE HORSES. **ACCENT: AMERICAN OR BRITISH.**

For the **ELVES** they are the First Born peoples of Middle-Earth. They're immortal, they are not subject to age or disease, but they can be slain or die or grief. They are the fairest of all earthly creatures, tall and slender, graceful but strong, resistant to the extremes of nature such as cold. Their senses, especially those of hearing and sight, are much keener than those of Men... THE ACTORS PLAYING ELVES WILL HAVE TO WEAR SOME PROSTHETIC MAKE-UP, MAYBE EARS AND CONTACT LENSES. **ACCENT: BRITISH**

For the **DWARVES** they are the short, stocky miners and battlers of Middle-Earth. Although about 4 feet in height, we think that casting a normal-sized person, and reducing them with CG, will give us greater casting options. Dwarves should have a likeable rough diamond quality. **ACCENT: BRITISH**
(Copyright 2003, BREAKDOWN SERVICES, LTD., All Rights Reserved)

[FRODO BAGGINS]   A Hobbit. 18-24 years old. Male. 5'4; - 5'9", normal build. Fine featured and good looking, Frodo is a natural leader. He is intelligent and carefree, with a roguish sense of humor and a disarmingly boyish charm. Frodo lives in the shadow of his famous adventurer uncle, Bilbo Baggins, and longs to have his own adventure beyond the bounds of the Shire. However, when confronted with the terrors of the real world Frodo starts to doubt his own abilities. It is testament to his courage and heart that, despite his misgivings and fears, he volunteers to take the One Ring to Mordor.

Frodo's struggle with the malicious influence of the Ring pushes him to the brink of paranoia and madness. By the end of his journey Frodo is hanging by a thread, his strength almost gone, his carefree spirit broken. The Frodo who returns to the Shire is humble, quiet, and haunted. Of all the characters in the story, Frodo has the most profound journey... LEAD ROLE. APPEARS IN PART ONE, PART TWO, AND PART THREE. **ACCENT: BRITISH**

[SAMWISE GAMGEE] A Hobbit. 25-30 years old. Male. 5'4" to 5'9". Stocky build. Practical and quiet, Sam is often the source of unwitting humor—although he is more astute than some give him credit for. He is unsophisticated, quick-tempered, and suspicious. Sam faces each new trial with a sometimes gloomy foreboding, but also a grim determination to see the job done. A humble gardener by trade, his intense loyalty to Frodo sees him rise to great acts of self-sacrifice and heroism. By the end of the story, Sam has grown in confidence and stature. His final parting with Frodo, although touched with sadness, also reveals the depth of understanding and wisdom Sam has acquired... SUPPORTING LEAD. APPEARS IN PART ONE, PART TWO, AND PART THREE. **ACCENT: BRITISH**

[MERIADOC (MERRY) BRANDYBUCK] A Hobbit. 18-24 years old. Male. 5'4" to 5'9". Normal build. Merry is more canny and knowing than the average Hobbit. A master prankster, Merry is usually able to talk his impetuous partner in crime, Pippin, into taking part in his schemes. Merry is quick-witted and resourceful, confident, and cheerful. He dreams of being heroic but in actual fact is not naturally brave, and manages to surprise even himself when he is finally called to do great deeds on the battlefield... A KEY PLAYER IN THE SUPPORTING CAST. APPEARS IN PART ONE, PART TWO, AND PART THREE. **ACCENT: BRITISH**

[PEREGRIN (PIPPIN) TOOK] A Hobbit. 18-20 years old. Male. 5'4" to 5'9". Normal Build. The youngest Hobbit, Pippin is impulsive,

outspoken, and a ball of energy. He is charming and fearless, but his lack of maturity and insight does tend to get him in trouble. Pippin is intrepid, mainly because he doesn't stop to think about danger, but also because he has a big heart. Despite thinking himself quite worldly, it is his innocent and trusting nature that endears him so readily to others. He is a natural comic... A KEY PLAYER IN THE SUPPORTING CAST. APPEARS IN PART ONE, PART TWO, AND PART THREE. **ACCENT: BRITISH.**

[BILBO BAGGINS]   A Hobbit. 55-years plus. Male. 5'4" to 5'9". Portly, compact. A true eccentric, who cares not a fig for the opinion of others, Bilbo is strong-minded, outspoken, and does not suffer fools gladly. He has a great and abiding love for his nephew, Frodo, of whom he is enormously proud. Unlike most Hobbits, Bilbo has a great love for adventure and travel, and given half a chance he'll talk endlessly about his youthful exploits. Bilbo has a wide mischievous streak and even at his age still enjoys playing tricks upon his neighbors and relatives. After Bilbo gives up the Ring he quickly ages, losing much of his energy and metal agility... APPEARS IN PART ONE AND PART TWO. THIS IS A CAMEO ROLE THAT WILL REQUIRE THE ACTOR TO BE IN NEW ZEALAND FOR APPROXIMATELY 4 WEEKS. **ACCENT: BRITISH.**
(Copyright 2003, BREAKDOWN SERVICES, LTD., All Rights Reserved)

[ARAGORN]   Human. 30-45 years old. Male. Ruggedly handsome leading man. Aragorn is our leading Human role. He is enigmatic, brooding, and intelligent. Aragorn carries an aura of concealed power and greatness about him, but also a deep sense of humanity and kindness. Aragorn goes through a great internal struggle in facing his destiny as King. Valiant, noble, and wry, he has never sought greatness and has an innate fear of the corrupting nature of power. Aragorn's noble lineage is initially hidden beneath the persona of "Strider," a mysterious ranger who is used to living rough and skilled in surviving in the wild. Aragorn is a skilled sword fighter… APPEARS IN PART ONE, PART TWO, AND PART THREE. **ACCENT: AMERICAN OR BRITISH. ALSO SUBMIT STAR NAMES.**

[GANDALF]   Human/Wizard. 55-plus years, male. IT IS ESSENTIAL THAT THE ACTOR WHO PLAYS GANDALF IS A CONFIDENT HORSE RIDER. Gandalf is a figure of great authority and warmth. He is a wise, far-seeing sage who dearly loves the good creatures of Middle-Earth, in particular, Hobbits. A young spirit trapped in an old body, Gandalf is frustrated by his failing memory and arthritic knees. He is an eccentric and has moments of quirky comedy. Gandalf is reinvented halfway through the story when he changes from "Gandalf the Grey" to "Gandalf the White." His age drops from 70ish to early 50s. The reborn Gandalf leads Gondor into war, but temporarily loses something of his old humanity and humor, becoming more formidable as a character… LEAD. APPEARS IN PART ONE, PART TWO, AND PART THREE. **ACCENT: AMERICAN OR BRITISH. ALSO SUBMIT STAR NAMES.**

[SARUMAN]   Human/Wizard. 60-plus years. Male. A melodic/hypnotic voice. Piercing eyes. Thin, tall, stooped. The key villain in the story. The leader of the Istari, the Wizards who offer counsel to the creatures of Middle-Earth, Saruman has immense stature and dignity. As the story unfolds we learn that he has been corrupted by greed for power and has betrayed his sacred duties. Where he was once noble and wise, he is now arrogant and cunning; duplicitous and self-serving… APPEARS IN PART ONE AND PART TWO. **ACCENT: AMERICAN OR BRITISH. ALSO SUBMIT STAR NAMES.**

[BOROMIR]   Human. 30-45 years old. Male. Strong, tall, thick-set. Boromir is the eldest son of Denethor, Steward of Gondor. Introverted and something of a loner, he has been oppressed by a domineering and violent father. Boromir is mistrustful of others, particularly

wizards, and regularly pours scorn on Gandalf. Boromir believes in the greatest of men, but he has no real belief in himself. The more likable side of his character is brought out by the Hobbits, whom he finds very endearing. Boromir is easily swayed by the power of the Ring, and under its influence he turns quite malicious. He does, however, come to see the error of his ways and very honorably redeems himself, dying a hero's death to save Merry and Pippin... MAJOR SUPPORTING ROLE. APPEARS IN PART ONE. **ACCENT: AMERICAN OR BRITISH. ALSO SUBMIT STAR NAMES.**

[DENETHOR]   Human. 50-70 years old. Male. A craggy, physical powerful man. Elderly but not frail. The Steward of Gondor, Denethor is a troubled man with a violent temper, prone to making irrational decisions. He is mistrustful, obsessive, domineering, and unreasonable. Denethor is ruler of Gondor, but he is acutely aware that the Steward is only the custodian of the throne, until the rightful king returns. Denethor does not accept this and resists the notion that one day the true king will return and take power from him. Denethor is a depressive, forecasting doom and destruction at every opportunity. He takes the loss of his son, Boromir, very badly, punishing his younger son, Faramir, for Boromir's death. In a moment of arrogance and despair, Denethor kills himself, in final and absolute abnegation of his responsibilities as Steward of Gondor... KEY SUPPORTING ROLE. APPEARS IN PART THREE. **ACCENT: AMERICAN OR BRITISH. PLEASE SUBMIT STAR NAMES.**
(Copyright 2003, BREAKDOWN SERVICES, LTD., All Rights Reserved)

[FARAMIR]   Human. 18-25. Male. Boyish, slim, handsome. Second son of Denethor, Steward of Gondor, Faramir has grown up in the shadow of his brother, the mighty Boromir. Reliable, intensely loyal to Gondor and its people, Faramir is adept at hiding the hurt and humiliation he feels when being ranted at by his deranged father. He is not serious or grim by nature, but he does have a premature weariness about him, as if for too long he was borne the weight of his father's problems. Above all, Faramir is extremely honorable and displays a wisdom that is well behind his years… KEY SUPPORTING ROLE. APPEARS IN PART THREE. **ACCENT: AMERICAN OR BRITISH. PLPEASE SUBMIT STAR NAMES.**

[THEODEN] Human. 50-plus, male. He is very much in the image of a Norse King with possibly a Nordic look. IT IS ESSENTIAL THAT THE ACTOR WHO PLAYS THEODEN IS A CONFIDENT HORSE RIDER. He is King of Rohan. Theoden is old beyond his years; ailing and distracted, he is under the influence of a cunning and manipulative advisor, called Wormtongue. It is only when Wormtongue is expelled that Theoden returns to his old self, shedding twenty years of decrepitude to once again assume the mantle of kingship… Theoden is a key supporting role. REQUIRED FOR PARTS ONE, TWO, AND THREE. **ACCENT: AMERICAN OR BRITISH. PLEASE SUBMIT STAR NAMES.**

[EOWYN] Human, 18-30, female. A Nordic warrior princess. Must be able to ride a horse and wield a sword. The niece of King Theoden, Eowyn is sometimes called the White Lady of Rohan—this is in part due to her paleness and her long fair hair, and in part to her solemn reserve, mistaken by some for coldness. She is beyond compare as a horsewoman, can wield a sword as well as any man, and is neither squeamish nor sentimental. She may also have a sharp tongue and a caustic wit, but shows great vulnerably when her feelings are moved. This is particularly the case with Aragorn, with whom she falls helplessly and hopelessly in love… Eowyn is a key supporting role, with a brief appearance in Part One, followed by a larger role in Parts Two and Three. **ACCENT: AMERICAN OR BRITISH. PLEASE SUBMIT STAR NAMES.**

[ARWEN] An Elf. 18-30, female. Slender, graceful, fine-featured. Will have to ride a horse and wield a sword. The Princess of Rivendell,

Arwen's beauty is legendary. An Elf, Arwen is, by virtue of birth, immortal. Everything about Arwen is "quick"—her fleetness, her smile, her temper, her understanding. She seems to enjoy playing against pre-conceptions of the classical serene Elven maiden. She dresses in armor, rides hell-for-leather and she gives her heart to a mortal man. Arwen's love for Aragorn is deep and abiding. She is prepared to give up her immortality and embrace death for him. But she also loves her father, the Lord Elrond, and it costs her greatly to defy him. Arwen's journey is towards a deeper understanding of the darkness and evil that exists in the world and a true understanding of what is means to be mortal... Arwen is the female romantic lead. APPEARS IN PARTS ONE, TWO, AND THREE. **ACCENT: BRITISH. PLEASE SUBMIT STAR NAMES.**

[LEGOLAS] An Elf. 25-35, male. Slim, graceful, handsome. A prince of the Wood Elves, Legolas is a deeply talented bowman, who can move with great stealth. Tall, slender, and fine-featured, Legolas is physically everything that Gimli the dwarf is not! Legolas sees Gimli as a dour, work-obsessed, and humorous old curmudgeon. It's the dynamic of the "odd couple": two opposites constantly bickering and bantering, each making jokes at the other's expense. But beneath the veneer of ironic humor, Legolas cares very much for those he has pledged to protect, and ultimately he and Gimli become fast friends... Legolas is a key supporting role in all three films. APPEARS IN PARTS ONE, TWO, AND THREE. **ACCENT: BRITISH. PLEASE SUBMIT STAR NAMES**.
(Copyright 2003, BREAKDOWN SERVICES, LTD., All Rights Reserved)

[ELROND] An Elf. 40-plus. Tall, slim, fine features. The Lord of the Elves of Rivendell and the father of Arwen, Elrond has great authority and wisdom, but also humility. He is something of a seer and is troubled by his daughter's love for the mortal, Aragorn, knowing as he does Aragorn's dark destiny. In a wider sense Elrond feels a great

BREAKDOWN SERVICES, LTD.
www.breakdownservices.com

Los Angeles	New York	Vancouver	London
(310) 276-9166	(212) 869-2003	(604) 943-7100	(01) 459-2781

The Link: www.submitlink.com

The information contained in this document is the exclusive property of Breakdown Services, Ltd. Any unauthorized reproduction, duplication, copying or use of the information contained herein, without prior written consent of Breakdown Services, Ltd., is strictly prohibited.

sadness that the age of the Elves is coming to a close—but he does not try to change this fact, accepting it as fate… Elrond is a cameo role with brief appearances in all three films. APPEARS IN PARTS ONE, TWO, AND THREE. **ACCENT: BRITISH. PLEASE SUBMIT STAR NAMES.**

[GIMLI]   A Dwarf. 30-50, male. A regular-sized person, but short and stocky with broad shoulders would be preferable. (C.G./bluescreen will be used to shrink size.) A pugnacious dwarf with a big heart, Gimli is brave and valiant; a warrior to the core, who lives by the warrior's code, he is loyal to the last. Gimli is a boisterous spirit who enjoys poking fun at the Elves, in particular Legolas. Gimli loves wine, women, and song and has a earthy sense of humor. Whilst hardly refined, he is capable of appreciating beauty— especially the beauty of well-hewn rock of the mines and tunnels made by his forebears…Gimli is a major supporting role. APPEARS IN PARTS ONE, TWO, AND THREE. **ACCENT: BRITISH.**

Kids Ruled "School"

School of Rock

Hollywood is famously a star-driven business in which name actors regularly command eight-digit salaries, plus a percentage of the back-end profits, and who just as regularly get director approval, casting approval, and, perhaps most significant of all, script approval. The industry trades are full of stories of actors' parts being beefed up, scaled down, reshot, re-edited, and otherwise tinkered with at the whim of the stars without whom their films wouldn't garner financing.

But how often does the script for a major studio film get rewritten for the sake of an unknown Chinese-American pianist, aged twelve, from Millington, New Jersey, who had not only never starred in a movie but had never even acted before?

This is just one instance in which the casting process for Paramount's 2003 film *School of Rock* had a direct impact on the film itself, as much as the other way around. Every year the industry launches its share of "cast-contingent" projects, either officially contracted as such (see the chapter on *Alias*) or unofficially dependent on finding exactly the right lead, often a relative unknown (see the chapter on *The Princess Diaries*).

In the case of *School of Rock*, the creative team—writer Mike White, director Richard Linklater, and producer Scott Rudin—signed on for a project that would rely almost entirely on the authenticity of its youth casting. For this story of a washed-up rocker, to be played by actor/musician Jack Black, teaching the basics of rock 'n' roll to a class full of classical musical prodigies at a posh private school, the mandate was clear from the outset.

"From Day One, we wanted kids who obviously had good personalities but who really were the real thing, in terms of [being] musicians and singers," says Ilene Starger (*Sleepy Hollow, Two Weeks Notice, The Parent Trap*), who was brought on as casting director in July, 2002, for a planned November shoot in New York—even before director Linklater had joined the project. "Scott [Rudin] knew that the more time we had, the better."

Starger works with her associate Janice Wilde and assistant Zoe Rotter from a sunny New York office in an unlikely industrial zone. They weren't the only casting professionals brought on board, though: Scouts were also hired in Detroit, Chicago, Minneapolis, Vancouver, Toronto, and San Francisco—nearly the whole country, although the New York-set film did preclude "people with thick Southern accents."

In Los Angeles, casting director Liz Lang Fedrick was hired to handle West Coast submissions. Like Starger, Fedrick notes that the film's unique casting challenges were budgeted into pre-production, and that it was clearly worth it.

"What's wonderful is when you have a producer who understands that in order to get the kind of cast that they got, they would [have to] spend both the money and the time searching for it," says Fedrick, who logged six weeks on her search. "Not many producers would pay for that. It really shows in quality of the cast when people pay for it."

Still, there was the natural fear that no amount of time might be sufficient.

"Initially, I have to say, we were all a little nervous," Starger admits. "It's hard enough to find kids who can hold their own on a screen, taking the music out of the equation. When we were all talking early on, and Rick and Scott were saying, 'Well, of course,

we really want kids who can play and sing, but at an expert level—
not just fake,' we were thinking, Oh my God—is that really possible? And honestly, we really didn't know going in. Would we actually be able to find kids who were that skilled?"

The immediate answer, the casting directors found, was yes and
no—and so the rewrites began. The initial script, and corresponding
Breakdown, sought children aged nine to eleven to play nine-year-
olds. The age requirement was the first thing to be changed.

"One of the things that we found out when we were talking to
music teachers was that it's hard...at that age, unless someone is
exceptionally gifted, because their fingers are still developing and
small," says Starger. "They felt that really, for prodigies, [it was]
better to up the age a bit."

And so White and Linklater agreed to change the age to eleven,
sending out a call for kids aged nine to twelve to play "ten or
eleven."

And then came the "Yuki" problem. In the original script, a
young Japanese-American "classical guitar prodigy" named Yuki is
appointed lead guitarist of the classroom rock band, though, as the
Breakdown read, "His real ambition is to get good grades and ultimately become a doctor." The final note: "His parents want no part
of Dewey," meaning Jack Black's character.

The hitch, as any suburban parent or teacher might be able to
tell you, is that guitar—even of the classical variety—is not typically the instrument of choice for young Asian-American prodigies.
More typical, the *School of Rock* casting directors found, was piano,
with other traditional orchestral instruments (strings, woodwinds)
a close second.

The original script had an overweight black girl, Lori, as the
band's pianist. But after searching the New York area, Starger and
her associates came across a Tennessee-based public radio program
called *From the Top*, which features performances by the best young
musicians from around the country. There they made a discovery
they couldn't let go, whether he fit the script or not.

"We found Robert Tsai, who is a brilliant, brilliant classical
pianist—I mean, we went to a concert of his at Lincoln Center when
were preparing the film," recalls Starger, still awed at the memory.

"He is someone who when he's an adult will just be, you know, at Carnegie Hall; I mean, he's a genius. As a person, he's very shy; he lives in New Jersey with his family, and music is his life. He's an incredibly smart, lovely boy. We auditioned him many times, and everybody kind of fell in love with him and thought, Well, he's great, but obviously his main instrument is piano..."

Again, it was back to the drawing board.

"The great thing about Rick [Linklater] and Mike [White] is that they were smart enough to know that if we found a kid who was really special who, let's say, didn't exactly fit the part as written, that they would tailor the script to that child," Starger says.

Fedrick agrees: "That's the most fun, when you have people around you who are just like, 'Whoa, I can see why you brought this person back. She doesn't fit any of the requirements, but we can completely see where you were going on that.' They open it up to that. And it's especially easy with children, because they either have it or they don't."

Still, the filmmakers wanted to keep one basic story element: that Dewey, a self-styled guitar "hero," would mentor a shy young guitarist whose parents are scornful of popular music. In other words, they couldn't just change Yuki to a pianist. So they created a character for Tsai: Lawrence, a quiet, sweet, bespectacled prodigy who, though he seems a little bewildered by rock music, is up for the dare Dewey gives the class.

This character sketch isn't too far from the real Robert, Starger explains.

"He comes from a very traditionalist [background in] classical music. I mean, I don't think he's someone who sits at the piano playing Doors music. In the film, he's playing electric piano, and as great as he is in the film, in terms of playing the piano, as I said, if you sat in a room with him—it barely even scratches the surface of his gift. So that was something for him that was a little bit of a challenge that he rose to magnificently, to play an instrument that he's not really in his daily life playing...and playing those kind of riffs."

If Tsai doesn't get the chance to show off the full range of his classical chops in the film, White did at least give him one of the film's signature lines: when Lawrence protests that he couldn't possibly be in a rock band, because, he says, "I'm not cool enough."

The inspired creation of Lawrence meant that other characters had to shift: The filmmakers still needed a young axe-slinger, and he wouldn't be Asian. And their chubby African-American piano prodigy would need a new job description.

From the rock capital of Detroit came eleven-year-old Joey Gaydos Jr., the son of a seasoned rock guitarist who fronted the hair-metal band The Weapons in the 1980s and played extensively with Motor City legend Cub Koda (of classic rockers Brownsville Station). Starger and associates found Gaydos through DayJams, a rock 'n' roll music camp with locations across the country. Despite his tender age, Gaydos was no neophyte; he reportedly received the gift of a guitar on his first birthday and began sitting in on his dad's gigs from the age of ten.

"Obviously it's in the genes, and he's been playing music since he was a baby, and he worships his dad," says Starger. Another element might have played a part, recalls Starger's associate, Janice Wilde: "Joey had his entire school praying—the nuns were saying prayers for him."

Divine intervention or not, screenwriter White tailored the part to Gaydos, changing "Yuki" to "Zack" but retaining the character arc, from shyness to relative coolness, and the crucial conflict of parental disapproval.

For the "chubby" Lori, the filmmakers dropped the piano and made her a singer—"an exceptionally talented singer who can really belt out a song," reads the Breakdown—and somewhere along the line changed her name to Tomika.

One thing they didn't change, though, was the following description: "shy, meek, heavyseat...very self-conscious..." Finding self-identified "overweight" performers, particularly young ones, is not always the easiest thing to pull off in a sensitive and upfront way (see the chapter on *Real Women Have Curves*).

Fedrick, whose office is based in image-conscious L.A., says that the filmmakers' main concern was to treat the film's young stars with respect, no matter the role's requirements.

"We didn't in any way want to affect them negatively at all, and we were dealing with really hard issues—you know, like being a nerd, and some of those kids *are* nerds, and being fat," says Fedrick. "That was one of the issues with [the character] Lori. We didn't wanna just hire a little girl who was chubby, because we didn't want children [in the audience] to think, 'That's fat.' So we really had to find an overweight little girl who had such an amazing talent [that] you absolutely see past it. Because that's the lesson [we] were trying to teach children—to see past the outside to the beauty and the talent within."

Explains Starger, "It was about...somebody who didn't necessarily fit the typical description of beauty, or somebody who feels that kids would make fun of her. And that's why initially [the character] didn't even volunteer that she had this amazing voice."

At the open call where Maryam Hassan, the nine-year-old charmer who would eventually nab the Lori/Tomika role, first appeared, Starger says she stood out in much the same way the character would in the film—reluctantly at first, but definitively once she opened her mouth.

"That was an awesome day," recalls Starger. "It was a rainy Saturday, I think, and we'd been casting the movie for a very long time, and we'd been looking for this part. We'd seen some good girls, but we didn't see anybody who was really overweight and/or who still looked the age. A lot of girls who were really overweight looked more like fourteen, fifteen.

"We had this open call on 42nd Street at a rehearsal studio, and she walked in, and we were all hopeful, because she looked great. And then she sang a cappella the first few lines of 'I Will Always Love You,' the Dolly Parton song. Again, she and most of these kids had never acted a day in their lives, not even in school plays. [Maryam] was obviously very, very shy, but she was so perfect in her shyness, and she's beautiful. And that voice just stopped us."

Along the lines of respecting kids' boundaries, there was the matter of casting the supporting character of Anuj, released in a Breakdown on October twenty-fifth. He's described as "an obsessive fan of musical theatre...[who] eventually becomes the band's wardrobe stylist or possibly its choreographer...a huge Bette Midler fan," to be played ideally by a "flamboyant, witty boy who has a beautiful Broadway-type voice and can sing 'Send in the Clowns.'"

The obvious stereotypically gay associations, laid on a bit thick in the Breakdown, are played gently for laughs in the film—as are the "job requirements" of a groupie, a post the attractive young Summer (Miranda Cosgrove) is assigned until she reads up on rock history and demands a more respectable post (Dewey makes her the band's manager).

For Anuj, Fedrick explains, the filmmakers were sensitive to a fault.

"I don't think you find a child that plays [gay]," she says. "What you do is you don't play that at all. You find a child who's got no problem dressing up—like when I was a kid with my little brother, he would just as often wanna be the bride as the groom. It was always just 'a flair for the dramatic.' When they're ten years old, that's all it is. There was nothing more. We don't want somebody to then say, 'Oh, that's the gay character.' He wasn't; he was just the one who may very well one day be Isaac Mizrahi."

Indeed, the PG-13 film deftly finesses the more adult connotations of sex, drugs, and rock 'n' roll.

"Those things were put to the side," concurs Fedrick, "so that is was just a fun movie. It was still entertaining for the adults, but at the children's level—especially the child actors' perceptions of themselves. We wanted that to remain pure."

TOO MUCH FUN

The search was exhaustive in the aforementioned Eastern and Midwestern cities. In L.A., Fedrick says, in addition to seeking talent from talent agencies, "We went to the Gospelfest and all the black churches trying to find Lori. We went to all the piano [teachers] in Orange County, in L.A. We called music teachers and pretended like we had children that we wanted to enroll. We went to all the conservatories."

Between the open calls and in-office auditions, Starger says, "We saw literally thousands of children."

The reward for this intensive searching, though, was a series of auditions that the casting directors still recall with an authentic

glow. While most in their profession enjoy the creativity and imme-
diacy of the audition process, the way Starger, her associates, and
Fedrick describe it, casting the children for *School of Rock* sounds
like the kind of job you can't believe you're getting paid to do.

"Really, for months, our life here was wall-to-wall children,
every single day," recalls Starger. "It was fun."

Concurs Wilde, her associate: "Some people think it's annoying;
I thought it was pretty inspiring."

"We loved it," says Starger. "Just the spirit and the sweetness."
And the stories start to pour out: "[There was] one girl we loved
who we unfortunately couldn't cast because she wasn't really
heavy—Dominique, who auditioned for the Tomika part. She was
just this adorable girl, and she loved Barbra Streisand. She came in
here and she sang, entirely a cappella, 'I'm the Greatest Star' from
Funny Girl."

Says Starger's assistant, Zoe Rotter, "It was amazing what everyone would pick. We had every single child, whether they were
singers or not, sing. So Angelo Massagli, who played Frankie in the
movie, came in and sang 'Crazy Train.'"

The range of material was indeed startling, says Starger. "These
little girls come in, very sophisticated, and they would sing everything from a Britney Spears song to 'Rose's Turn' from *Gypsy*. We
were hysterical—you know, they come in and sing these torch
songs." Starger relates that Aleisha Allen, who ended up being cast
in a small part in the film, offered a rendition of Alicia Keys' song
"Why Don't You Call Me No More," complete with "the moves and
everything."

Wilde also noticed how music-savvy some of the young performers were—and not just about the Top 40.

"It was great to see kids come in and have Ramones T-shirts on,
and girls who were loving Debbie Harry," Wilde recalls. "Blondie
was mentioned many times—little kids, nine-year-olds, saying,
'Blondie is my hero.'"

Another contrast the casting staff found memorable was
between adults and youngsters.

"We were having auditions concurrently for other parts in the
film, so we'd be having a lot of adult guys come in to play band

members, and they'd bring their instruments," Starger recalls. "They'd be sitting out [in the lobby], and we'd be in an audition, and the door would be shut. We had drums in there; Joey came with his guitar. And these thirty-year-old guys would be, 'Wow, they're really good!' And then they'd see this little kid coming out."

Wilde chimes in: "We knew we hit something when the neighbors came and knocked on the door, complaining. It was like we were in college."

Inside the room, though, Starger and her colleagues were often genuinely awed by the young performers' spirit and guts.

"It's funny—in the movie, it's so clear that these kids are really talented," says Starger. "And yet when you're one-on-one with them in a room, the force of it coming out of these little kids—I mean, they are *young*. It's awesome, amazing."

Of course, there's a flip side to this youthful enthusiasm, as Starger admits.

"It's hard enough to have to turn people down, but some of these kids would come in and say, 'Well, when are callbacks?' And of course it's always the people who say that who are not gonna get the part. But we wanted them to leave here feeling really good."

As Fedrick puts it: "What we tried to do with all the children, since they were non-pros, is to make them think that each step they get to, that was *it*, that was the best, and that they should be so proud of themselves that they got that far. Because even with adults, you get to that point [in auditions] where it's either you or the other guy, and you know, it's a lot of money, a lot of prestige—it's a big fat hairy deal. To miss out on that can be so devastating if not handled it in the right way."

In callbacks, director Richard Linklater, himself the parent of a young child, was a model of graciousness, according to Starger.

"He's just so lovely and sensitive," she says. "From the minute these kids started coming in—we would bring back the good ones for him, the ones that we really felt strongly about—he never spoke down to them; he took them very seriously. He never condescended. He just made everybody feel: Wow, you're cool, you're good."

Those who made it to the final callback won't soon forget it, as Fedrick explains.

"At the end, [Jack Black] did a special read with the children. We only brought back two or three of each category of the kids to do that, and the kids were so excited. We had seen almost all non-pros, but even the kids who were pros, you know, they're nine, ten years old still—and I had no idea what a huge fan base Jack has among ten-year-olds.

"So one of the funny things that we did—it actually kind of embarrassed Jack to do it. The kids played guitar with Jack, and we took a Polaroid of them playing guitar together, and then Jack signed it for them, so they could take it away. One little boy who didn't end up getting [the part] framed [the photo] in his room, and he could take it to school, and say, 'No, look, I *did* go and audition. Here's a picture of me and Jack and he signed it.'"

While the initial auditions were based on appearance, demeanor, and musical ability, subsequent callbacks focused on acting ability and on the coherence of the ensemble—to see if these kids, in more than one sense, could play well with others.

"It was a long process, very painstaking," Starger says. "We brought kids back a lot, just to put it together. They came back here five times, some of them. Because we had to be sure. When you put any kind of a cast together, you're mixing and matching: Does this one look like this one? But especially in this case, it was so crucial that every single person just complemented the other."

One danger of such extensive auditions and callbacks is that an actor, let alone a child actor, can freeze up and get too "set" in his reading.

"This is another fine line; we always tell them, 'Don't go home and over-rehearse,' because we don't want that sing-songy quality," Starger explains. "It's very tough with child actors; you have to make it sound natural and real. And anyway, we wanted to avoid that. We wanted kids who looked like real kids; we did not want actor-looking children."

This was another of the film's central casting mandate: realism, not only in the playing of instruments but in the playing of the parts. It's a paradox many young performers and their parents come up against all too often, after training and primping and getting themselves agents: Casting directors, and the directors and producers who hire them, don't want "actor-y" kids, they want "real" kids. Of course, the best acting is rooted in reality, effacing technique or flash so we forget we're watching a performance. It's just that very often, with kids, the industry seeks, and often finds, young non-actors to do this "non-acting."

"We wanted kids who as much as possible were real kids," Starger says. "We always want a realism and a non-showbizzy-fake kind of kid."

That, and the requirement for genuine musicianship, were the reasons Starger found many of *School of Rock*'s stars off the beaten track: Robert Tsai in suburban New Jersey, Joey Gaydos Jr. outside Detroit, and Kevin Clark, who hails from Chicago, as the rambunctious young drummer Freddy. So it's not surprising that for the young ensemble's crucial non-musical part—Summer, the band's precocious manager—an impish, raven-haired beauty named Miranda Cosgrove was found in L.A. Though at nine, Cosgrove turned out to be the youngest of the children on the set, she had the most acting experience; her career began at age three.

It doesn't count as a big script change, but Summer was envisioned differently than the preternaturally wise character Miranda brought to the screen.

"It's funny, because initially they wanted blonde—they envisioned Summer as being a little picture-perfect blonde girl," Starger recalls, noting the "blonde, privileged" description in the Breakdown. "But Miranda just leapt out; she's gorgeous, and she just had the perfect inflections."

NOT SO SHY

One pressure that's often brought to bear on casting directors is the "name game": Sure, the studio suits say, we want the best actor for the part, but would it kill you to give one of the Culkin kids a call?

"Did we check out the Haley Joel Osments of the world?" Starger asks rhetorically. "I mean, we checked them out. But it was so much about...kids who could really play. In the case of [Summer], who was the one person in the film who didn't have to play [an instrument], we looked at people like Dakota Fanning—she was way too young—or Emily Osment. That's part of your job in casting, to be really thorough."

Fedrick adds that casting non-stars for the kids made sense because it "fit the theme of the whole piece, which was: You don't have to look like the world says you have to look in order to be a success. That's one of the most beautiful things. Take Jack Black: Who would think he's a movie star, who would think he can get movies made? Nobody. But he can. Because he has irrepressible spirit, and he has irrepressible talent, and he believed and he did it."

Though few of the students in *School of Rock* had acting experience, it's not as if they'd never gotten up in front of people to perform. As Janice Wilde puts it, "If somebody's used to getting up in front of an audience anyway as a musician, then they're not so gunshy about getting in front of an audience or a camera. They have their sea legs, so to speak; they can sort of think on their feet."

Still, with so much riding on these performers, the filmmakers not only gave the casting directors plenty of time and resources to find the right kids—they also planned time to get the kids ready for their close-ups.

"We had built into the budget and the schedule, which is very unheard of for a film, for the kids [to have] almost four weeks of rehearsal time, prep time, to make them really feel comfortable with each other, with the instruments, with Jack," Starger says. "So that by the time they got out on the set, they would know their lines, they would have blocked it and rehearsed it. That was a luxury to have that time."

One side benefit of casting non-pros is that the cliché of the "stage parent"—the Mama Roses who are pushing their children to compete by any means necessary—didn't surface as frequently during the *School of Rock* process as it otherwise might.

"We had a couple of unpleasant experiences, I would say— cases where it's so clear that the mothers are so nakedly ambitious and will do anything to get their child this job—but they were probably two in the midst of thousands," says Starger.

Says her associate, Janice Wilde: "They're usually women or men who wanted to do it themselves and weren't successful, so the children are gonna do it for them."

Starger relates one audition tale worthy of the Bravo reality series *Showbiz Moms & Dads*.

"We had one very bad experience where a really talented, beautiful little girl just sort of broke down sobbing," Starger recounts. "And I said to her mother, 'I think you should take her home; don't push her if she doesn't want it.' And the mother actually got angry, as if we were keeping her child from her chance. She kept saying, 'Oh no, she's OK, she can do it.' I mean, this little girl was literally crouched in the corner, sobbing. And that's something that you just don't wanna see."

More common on the *School of Rock* auditions, Starger relates with relief, were the well-adjusted kids who would show up with their parents and brothers and sisters to auditions.

"Most of these kids were not only children, so a lot of them bring the whole family. They live in the suburbs, they play sports. In a certain way, they think this is really exciting, but they also do other things, so it doesn't just take them over."

Indeed, Starger, who has cast her share of films featuring young performers—*The Parent Trap*, *Three Men and a Little Lady*—believes that the healthiest child actors are the ones who work less.

"I always say, if a kid wants to do this, and they can do maybe one movie a year, great," Starger advises. "But put them back in their regular school, let them hang out with their friends. We were teasing all the moms, when the movie was wrapping and they were going home, back to Chicago and wherever, 'Well, when he gets home, he's still going to have to take the trash out.' I mean, it's fun to be on a movie set, and it's fun to have somebody bring you a bagel, but at the end of the day, you've still gotta clean your room."

Wilde recalls a visit she made to the set, where she witnessed director Richard Linklater giving the kids a kind of pep talk: "He took them aside one day and said, 'Your friends back home are not going to understand what you're going through, and don't try and make them. Don't go back and say, "Oh, I was in this movie," like a big shot, because you're just gonna get tweaked for that. Just keep each other's phone numbers so you can keep in touch with each other.'"

And they have, Starger says. On her desk, in fact, sits a card from Jordan Claire-Green, a young blonde who played Michelle in the movie.

"They've all stayed in touch, they all email each other, they became really good friends," Starger says. "Robert became really good friends with Kevin, the cool kid, the handsome drummer. On paper, they're as different as kids could be: Kevin is hip, cool, girls follow him everywhere. But it was great, because Kevin looked out for Robert, and in a way gave him some cool. And yet I think all of the kids were really impressed with Robert's seriousness and musical ability and work ethic.

"I'm making it sound like it was a total lovefest, but it really was. It was a really positive experience."

And not only for the young performers, Starger says. For her and her office, and for the offices across the country, *School of Rock* represents a big job well done.

"When you're looking for forty-year-old leading men, it's a fairly finite pool," Starger explains. "But when someone says to you, 'Go find those fifteen children who are musical prodigies,' there's a sense that the world is your oyster, and the longer you keep looking, the more you may find. We may see something in somebody right away, but you still have to go through a very laborious process to make everybody feel—understandably so—comfortable that this is truly the best choice. Because there's lot riding on it; obviously movies are very costly, and with kids, frankly, or anybody who's never acted before, you don't entirely know until you actually get them before a camera—what if the person freezes? We audition people all the time, both adults and kids, who are so nervous that it's clear to us that if you put them next to a movie star, they're not going to be able to do it."

Along similar lines, Wilde effuses: "Robert Tsai, the pianist that they changed the script for—his mother put him in front of the piano to keep him busy while she was doing her house chores, and it turned out that he took to it, and started playing at Lincoln Center. He was a rarity. You know, we were sent out to find the rare birds in the world. It's wonderful when you get something like that, because it's a challenge, as opposed to just finding the same people over and over again to play the same roles. You know, in a lot of movies we go to to today, you know exactly what's gonna happen because of who's cast in it: Julia Roberts is gonna get the guy. And in this case, you don't know what's gonna happen, necessarily."

Fedrick, a veteran of youth casting, is happy to be part of a small cadre of professionals who relish the challenge.

"Nobody wants to do kids, because they're new every single time, and it's a lot of work," Fedrick says. "But I love it."

Summing up what was clearly a once-in-a-lifetime ride for all involved, Starger says, "We look back on it with pride and affection, because you get something from just talking to kids—their spirit, and just the bravery, for anybody to come in and just start belting out a song or plug in a guitar. That's an amazing thing."

(File: 0812f03-rhm) L SAN DIEGO
(Original 0719n11-em) N, L,
CHI, FL, EVERYWHERE
PARAMOUNT PICTURES
"SCHOOL OF ROCK"
FEATURE FILM

DEL'D IN LA Tue., Aug. 13, 2002, Vol. 2002, #0813
Producer: Scott Rudin
Director: TBD
Writer: Mike White
Casting Director: Ilene Starger
Start: Early–Mid November 2002
Location: New York

SEND ALL SUBMISSIONS
IMMEDIATELY TO:

LIZ LANG FEDRICK–KIDS SEARCH

PLEASE NOTE: WE DO NOT VALIDATE PARKING AT LANTANA.

Previous breakdown released in Los Angeles July 22, 2002.

PLEASE NOTE: Children submitted must be available from early-mid October 2002 through February 2003. Film will shoot in New York State.

STORYLINE: Down and out rocker Dewey Finn (Jack Black) has been fired from his band, is deeply in debt, and is practically friendless. When he hears of a Battle of the Bands contest sponsored by a local radio station, Dewey is determined to win the prize money and turn his life around. None of Dewey's peers want to be in a band with him; one night, by chance, he hears 9-year-old guitar prodigy Yuki Takeuchi play. Yuki's a student at a prestigious private grade school, which prepares very young minds for Ivy League colleges. In order to get close to Yuki, Dewey poses as a substitute 4th grade teacher at the school, and unbeknownst to the parents and school personnel, decides to form a rock band with Yuki and the other student in the class.

NOTE: Except where noted, please submit actors of all ethnicities for the following roles:

[Yuki] 9-11 to play 9 years old. Asian to play Japanese. Shy and unpopular, Yuki is a stunning classical guitar prodigy whose personality blossoms when he is appointed lead guitarist in the band. However, although Yuki enjoys guitar, and his new popularity, his real ambition is to get good grades and ultimately become a doctor. His parents want no part of Dewey. Guitar experience helpful…

[SUMMER] 9-11 to play 9 years old. Summer is the classic teacher's pet and enjoys being in control and in charge of everything. She is blonde, privileged, precocious, and bossy. At the top of her class, she enjoys keeping tabs on the rest of the kids. She is immediately suspicious of Dewey and his unusual teaching methods…

[FREDDY] 9-11 to play 9 years old. Freddy has a short attention span and is very hyper. He is a mischievous gremlin who would probably be expelled if it weren't for his father's donations to the school. Dewey harnesses Freddy's energy and boosts his self-esteem by appointing him drummer of the band. Please submit actors with drumming experience who are very physical and can sing a bit…

[LORI] 9-11 to play 9 years old. Lori is a shy, meek, overweight girl who is a very talented pianist. Her mother is constantly calling her "fat" and telling her that she'll be denied opportunities because of her size. Dewey empathizes with Lori, and urges her to follow in the footsteps of Aretha Franklin and Mama Cass. Because of Dewey, Lori starts believing in her talent and herself. Please submit chubby girls who can play the piano.

[DEREK] 9-11 to play 9 years old. He is put on security detail. He and the others on security keep a lookout for teachers at the school to make sure no one outside the class knows about the band. Derek sings a bit of a Nirvana song at one point…

NOTE: Please submit all children (legal 9 to 11) with any special musical ability, even if they do not fit the character descriptions.

(File: 1024f03-iam) L
PARAMOUNT PICTURES
"SCHOOL OF ROCK"
FEATURE FILM

DEL'D IN NY Fri., Oct. 25, 2002, Vol. 2002, #1025
Producer: Scott Rudin
Director: Richard Linklater
Writer: Mike White
Casting Director: Ilene Starger
Casting Associate: Janice Wilde
Casting Assistant: Zoe Rotter
Start: Approx. Nov. 25, 2002 (with early Nov. rehearsal)

WRITTEN SUBMISSIONS ONLY TO: ILENE STARGER CASTING

STORYLINE: Down-and-out rocker Dewey Finn (Jack Black) has been fired from his band, is deeply in debt, and is practically friendless. In order to pay his rent, Dewey poses as his roommate, who is a substitute teacher, and begins teaching a 5th grade class. Hoping to win prize money offered at a local band contest, Dewey decides to form a rock band with the kids in the class. He must do this in secret so that the parents and school personnel know nothing of his plan...

[LORI] 9-12 to play 10 or 11. 4'4" to 5'. Lori is a shy, meek, heavyset girl; an exceptionally talented singer who can really belt out a song. She is very self-conscious due to her weight, and Dewey helps draw her out by encouraging her to sing and eventually strut her stuff. Think a 10-11 year old Mama Cass, Aretha Franklin, Jennifer Holliday, etc. Please submit all ethnicities...

[ANUJ] 9-12 to play 10 or 11. 4'4" to 5'. An obsessive fan of musical theatre. Anuj eventually becomes the band's wardrobe stylist or possibly its choreographer. He is a huge Bette Midler fan. Seeking a slightly flamboyant, witty boy who has a beautiful Broadway type voice and can sing "Send in the Clowns." Please submit all ethnicities...

Challenging "Curves" Ahead

Real Women Have Curves

"I think that I shall never see/Any Chicanos on TV," goes an old song by Lalo Guerrero. While networks and cable channels have made some progress in diversifying their casts, and even their corporate offices, Guerrero still wouldn't have much to watch today apart from ABC's not-exactly-gritty *The George Lopez Show*. And if Guerrero were looking for a realistic representation of Chicano culture on the boob tube, rather than just a few brown faces, he'd be channel-surfing for a long time.

That is, unless he happened upon a rerun of the HBO-produced film *Real Women Have Curves*, which had a theatrical release in 2002 before airing on the cable netlet. This modest, affecting coming-of-age drama, based on a play by Josefina Lopez, is resolutely set in East Los Angeles, among a multi-generational working-class family. The matter-of-fact authenticity of the film's setting has a lot to do with the film's casting, which presented numerous challenges and required an extensive search to find the film's lead, a high school senior named Ana, described in the original Breakdown as "outspoken and conflicted...must be plump."

It was a challenge the film's casting directors actively sought out.

"We were very aware of the project," says Maria E. Nelson, sitting in the small New York office she shares with Ellyn Long Marshall under the company name the Orpheus Group. "It was in the theatre pipeline, and so we kept tabs on it. So when we heard it was going to be done, we said, 'This is a project that we're actually actively gonna go after.'"

"Obviously they wanted an L.A. casting director," Marshall recalls. "But we were insistent."

"We said, 'No, we are the people to do it, and we will do whatever needs to be done,'" Nelson says.

The first thing they had to do was move to L.A. in the summer of 2001. And though their stay would last long enough to do a thorough search—and not only for the part of Ana—it's not as if these two were strangers to the Latino talent pool they found out West.

"The reality is that we have an incredible vocabulary of Latino actors," says Nelson, a former agent, who hails originally from Costa Rica. Indeed, she and Marshall got their start as casting directors at INTAR, a venerable Latino performing arts institution in New York. "A lot of the Latino actresses are now in California. They made this exodus quite a few years ago—they all have series. So it was very easy for us. We got to L.A. and we're like, Where's this one? Where's this one? We had a family already."

The family did grow, however. By definition the young lead, Ana, would likely be played by an actress with little or no track record on either coast. Nelson and Marshall would have to find her.

"We scoured Los Angeles," Nelson recalls. "We said to HBO from the very beginning, 'These people are not sitting home waiting for their agents to call them. It's just not gonna happen.' HBO knew that, so they said, 'You have to go out there in the community. That's why we hired you, because that's been your experience.'"

Indeed, the biggest feather in Orpheus' cap was discovering the extraordinary Michelle Rodriguez for the New York-based *Girlfight*—a feat they were able to accomplish by doing extensive searching in that city's Latino community. That Nelson is bilingual doesn't hurt.

"As long as you speak Spanish, and I do, and you're able to really communicate and develop a level of trust, you can move through the community much easier," Nelson says.

For *Real Women*, Marshall and Nelson hit schools—particularly English classes, because "Ana has very good English, and she had to be very bright," as Nelson puts it—and youth groups. But by far the most memorable day of casting on the film was a huge open call for the part of Ana at East L.A.'s Plaza de la Raza.

"The stories that these girls came in with—some brought me to tears, about their leaving their country and coming here," Marshall recalls. "They got up on the stage and talked as long as they wanted to. For me, it was a total education."

"It was probably one of the most extraordinary castings we've ever done," Nelson concurs, putting the count of young women seen at between 200 and 250. "I put the camera on and just let it run. It was a mind-blowing experience."

As the film's title and the Breakdown for Ana suggest, the film's realism extends to the delicate matter of girth. The Breakdown descriptions for Ana, for her mother, Carmen, and for her sister, Estela, all use the word "plump." This is not, to put it gently, a category that is on the minds of most talent agents, not to mention the film business as a whole.

"We work in a cosmetic industry," Nelson says. Which means, for instance, that there aren't a lot of larger girls with professional representation. "Agents don't have fat girls," as Marshall puts it.

Even so, the word "plump"—as opposed to "overweight" or "fat"—was not chosen lightly.

"We saw certain young ladies who were extremely large, and you have to be careful with that—that sort of takes it into another space," Nelson says. "That enters the other realm of...*large.*"

In fact, there are two characters in the Breakdown referred to as "large": Pancha and Dona, both seamstresses at the dress shop run by Ana's sister, Estela. These characters, along with a few other average-shaped Latinas, have a memorably affirmative scene late in the film, when Ana takes off her shirt due to the sweltering heat, inspiring the rest of her co-workers to strip to their skivvies and glory in their real, un-nipped and un-tucked bodies.

But the character of Ana herself, though she's constantly nagged by her mother about her weight, was intended to be what is what is often euphemistically called "full-figured." The title, after all, says "curves," not "curve." In fact, another Breakdown for Ana was released a few weeks after the initial notice, with added explanation. After the sentence "must be plump," a parenthetical definition was included, in bold type: "full figure, curvy, voluptuous."

All these considerations, on top of Ana's ethnicity and bilingualism, spelled a sizeable casting hurdle. As Marshall sums up: "That combination—a teenager who's heavy and yet has enough self-confidence to carry a film—was a real challenge."

COMING TO AMERICA

Actually, Nelson and Marshall saw the girl they would eventually cast as Ana in their first week on the job. An associate producer told them about a promising youngster she knew who was in New York at a summer theatre camp. The casting directors, always impressed by a teen with a commitment to theatre, called and coached young America Ferrera over the phone.

"We said to her, 'Put yourself on tape, this is what we want you to do,'" Nelson recalls. "The tape came, we looked at her, and from the minute we put the tape in and saw her, we said, 'This is the girl.'"

Then why did the search for the perfect Ana last, by Nelson and Marshall's estimation, three months?

"It's a little scary for a film company to actually in the first week look at somebody and say, 'This is the girl,'" Nelson explains. "HBO said, 'No, you're gonna go and look.'"

The search took them as far afield as Texas. Marshall remembers only "maybe one" other serious contender for the role. She was younger—"and bigger," Nelson adds—than Ferrera. "She was very good, very talented, and HBO liked her," Marshall recalls.

Finally, though, Nelson says, "We kept coming back to America. She really stood on her own. It was scary for [the producers], but in retrospect, she really had everything that it took, and we knew it from the first time she came in."

They also could tell by her reading with Lupe Ontiveros, the casting directors' early favorite for the part of Ana's feisty mother, Carmen. The young Ferrera was unfazed by the older actress's chops.

"Lupe came over and whispered to me, 'This girl is good,'" Marshall recounts. "She stood right up against her, and Lupe is rough—she's a tough cookie."

Indeed, the Breakdown describes Carmen as "sharp-tongued...uneducated but proud...the gossip queen of the barrio." It is she who calls Ana "gordita" throughout the film, which the sub-titles translate as "fatty." Though Nelson and Marshall say they read several other women for the part, this would seem to have been another producer-placating measure; Ontiveros owned the part from early on, and it's impossible to picture anyone else in the role.

Less easy to fill was the role of Estela, Ana's self-sufficient older sister, who has the enterprising spirit to open her own dress shop but often lacks the confidence to manage a crew of willful women, including her own mother and sister. The Breakdown describes her as "29...well groomed and well put together.... Artistic, not married."

"That was a very difficult role, and we were going crazy," Marshall recalls. "It was the last role, and we still hadn't seen any-body who was right. A friend of ours who's a manager called. I said, 'We cannot find this role,' and she said, 'You know, I have a friend—she hasn't been acting.' She was dealing with a lot of per-sonal stuff for a few years."

The actress was Ingrid Oliu, a strikingly poised, self-possessed woman who had had a memorable role in *Stand and Deliver* but hadn't acted much since.

"We brought her in and we just fell in love with her," Marshall says. Still, they felt Oliu needed some coaching to convince the pro-ducers—a job most casting directors will tell you is particularly sat-isfying, as it essentially fulfills the "director" part of their title.

"Once we met [Ingrid], we knew that she was the person," Nelson says. "So our job was, How do we make this happen?"

"[The producers] wouldn't have bought it just off the initial tape," Marshall explains. "She hadn't worked in a while and she didn't have the confidence. But the woman is brilliant."

"So we called her that night and said, 'Listen, Ingrid, you want this role?'" Nelson recalls. "'This is what you're gonna have to do, this is how you're gonna have to dress.'"

"'How you've got to fix your hair,'" Marshall chimes in.

Another audition with Nelson and Marshall's notes, and Oliu had the part.

REAL MEN, TOO

For the film's male roles, the Orpheus casting directors looked in Mexico—an eye-opening window into a parallel acting universe at once very familiar and quite apart from the Hollywood scene.

"That was an education for me," Marshall says of their dip into the Mexican talent pool. "They have amazing careers and we don't know about it here in this country. It's like a whole different world. The acting style in some cases was so different."

Ultimately the only actor they cast from Mexico was Felipe de Alba, who plays Ana's charming, tender grandfather, described in the Breakdown as "a dreamer."

"My heart—what an incredible actor," Nelson raves. "He works a lot in Mexico, on the big films. He's got an incredible résumé. He's based in Mexico; his management is in Mexico and also in New York."

They had hoped to cast the role of Ana's father Raul, described memorably in the Breakdown as "a Mexican John Wayne," with a Mexican national. But it was partly the complications of bringing foreign actors to the States the play just one role that foreclosed this prospect. It was also a matter of having an even better choice right here.

"I've always loved Jorge Cervera," Nelson says of the tall, broad actor who got the role and played it with lumbering gravitas and unmistakeable warmth. "I actually traveled with his picture from New York. I've always kept it with me, thinking, 'One of these days, I'm going to be able to use him for something.' And in L.A., they were talking about the dad, and I said, 'You have got to look at Jorge.' So I actively went and tracked him down and called him. I was determined that he was going to be the person."

The part of Ana's encouraging high school teacher, described as "liberal, idealistic, proper," went to George Lopez, who had not yet landed his eponymous TV show but was a "name" in the Latino community for a popular radio show and his standup work. And for the part of "Jacob," Ana's high school boyfriend, described in the

Breakdown as a "Jewish American...nerdy good kid who wants to rebel," the casting directors found an impish young man named Brian Sites, and the character's name was changed to Jimmy.

"Brian won our hearts the first day," Maria recalls with a laugh. She says that as she panned the camera down to take him in on that first audition, she noticed something peculiar. "He came in his slippers—his bedroom slippers—to audition! We had to say: 'Brian, are those your slippers?' But we knew; he had that look of wonder. He's extremely bright and extremely tuned in. You look at Brian's big blue eyes, and you just melt. He's a sunny actor."

Whether America would respond the same way was the big question.

"Of course we were very nervous the first time they read together," Nelson recounts. "We said, 'We hope that the chemistry works.' They took one look at each other, and it was instant like."

Marshall says that one of her office staff had called it early on.

"Our assistant on the project—she's from Venezuela, very heavy accent—she had this thing about Brian and America from the very beginning," Marshall says. "She put up pictures of the two of them together, and said: 'That's who's gonna do it.'"

ON THE GROUND

Clearly, casting is in large part a matter of intuition, of following one's gut—and following through. Nelson and Marshall say they usually get their sense of a film's spirit from the director.

"We really align ourselves with the director closely when we're working on a project," Nelson explains. "We are his ears, we are his heart, and so we have to connect. Once we connect with that, then we're able to really do our job. Because we have to get into his head, or her head, and see what they're seeing, so that we're able to give it to them."

Real Women's director, Patricia Cardoso, not only did her homework—she included the film's craftspeople in her research from early on.

"It's about vision—everybody had a vision for this," Nelson recalls. "When Brigitte Brocht, the production designer, came in, the following morning she got to the studio really early, and set the room up—she began to transform the office with all of the paraphernalia that would be Mexican. She put candles in every room. She transformed herself to that world—everybody did. And we really fed off each other."

The film's director of photography, Jim Denault, even helped Nelson and Marshall set up the camera and lights for their auditions—an extra touch that could only happen with a small crew.

"It was important for all of us to really connect," Nelson continues. "So we were all on the same floor in the same office building. And you begin to establish this bond, not only for yourself but for the film."

"It shows in the film," Marshall avers.

Real women, indeed.

 Los Angeles   New York   Vancouver   London
(310) 276-9166 (212) 869-2003 (604) 943-7100 (01) 459-2781

BREAKDOWN SERVICES, LTD.
www.breakdownservices.com   The Link: www.submitlink.com

(File: 0702f05-lkm) L	***DEL'D IN LA Tue., July 3, 2001, Vol. 2001, #0703***
(P. 0702n03-em) L,	Producer: George La Voo, Effie T. Brown
(P: 0621n08-em, 0619n03-em) N	Co-Producer: Marilyn Atlas
REAL WOMEN HAVE CURVES, INC.	Director: Patricia Cardoso
"REAL WOMEN HAVE CURVES"	Writer: Josefina Lopez and George La Voo
FEATURE FILM	Casting: Orpheus Group, Inc.
SEE NOTE BELOW	(Maria E. Nelson, Ellyn Long Marshall)
	Shoot: 8/13
	Location: Los Angeles, CA

ALL SUBMISSIONS TO:

"REAL WOMEN"
ORPHEUS GROUP CASTING

SPECIAL NOTE: Breakdown Service has been unable to verify the union status of this feature film. We have been assured by the producers of this project that they intend to file papers and comply with all union requirements. Breakdown Services recommends that talent representatives perform "due diligence" prior to submitting any union actors.

Previous Breakdowns have been released in NY.

[ANA] 18, Mexican-American. Must be plump. A school clown. Outspoken and conflicted. Should she follow the dreams of her traditional mother, or break away to make a new life for herself? Speaks English and Spanish...

[CARMEN] 47–55, Mexican. Ana's sharp-tongued mother. Must be plump. Uneducated but proud. Gossip queen of the barrio. Has a talent for story-telling. Speaks English and Spanish...

[ESTELA] 29, Mexican-American. Sister of Ana, daughter of Carmen. Plump, well-groomed and well put together. Owner of a small dress factory in East L.A. and employs all these women. Artistic, not married. Speaks English and Spanish...

[PANCHA] 40s–50s. Mexican. Large woman who is very mellow, but very quick with the tongue. Speaks English and Spanish. Natural comic timing...

[ROSALI] 30s. Mexican-American. Skinny but thinks she's fat. Always on a diet. Speaks English and Spanish. Naturally comedic...

[NORMA] 20s. Mexican. Traditional. Nervous and sweet and a hard worker. Speaks English and Spanish...

[DONA GORGONIA] 40s–50s. Mexican. A large woman. Eccentric housewife. Former circus performer. Speaks English and Spanish...

[RAUL] 47–60, Mexican. Father of Ana and Estela, husband of Carmen. A Mexican John Wayne. Speaks English and Spanish...

[GRANDFATHER MIGUEL] 70s. Mexican. A dreamer. Simple, uneducated, has difficulty walking after a life of hard labor in the fields. Adores story-telling. Speaks English and Spanish...

[MR. GUZMAN] 30s. Mexican-American. High school teacher. Liberal, idealistic, proper. Speaks English and Spanish...

[JACOB] 18. Jewish-American. Secretly dating Ana. Well-educated, well-mannered. A nerdy good kid who wants to rebel. Speaks English...

[JUAN JOSE] Teenager. Mexican. Sings, plays guitar. Juan Martin's best friend. Longs for the past and for home in Mexico. Speaks English and Spanish...

[JUAN MARTIN] Teenager. Mexican. Sings, plays guitar. Juan Jose's best friend. Has hope for the future and life in El Norte. Speaks English and Spanish...

[PATTY]   Teenager. Mexican-American. Missed a chance for education and started a family already as a young teen. Street smart...

[MRS. GLITZ]   40s–50s. European-American. Crass businesswoman, too sophisticated for words...

"Princess" Seeks
Gorgeous Goofball

The Princess Diaries

"Here's the thing: pretty and funny and a good actress—that's a hard combination," says casting director Lisa Miller Katz (*Everybody Loves Raymond*). "'God doesn't give with both hands' is the saying."

This "triple threat" requirement—beauty, comic talent, and film-carrying power—was easily the biggest challenge for Marcia Ross, senior vice president of feature film casting at Disney, when she set out in 2000 to find the teenage lead for director Garry Marshall's *The Princess Diaries*. Gina Wendkos' script was a contemporary ugly-duckling fable about an awkward high school girl, Mia, who discovers that her estranged father is prince of an obscure (and fictional) European kingdom called Genovia, and must be given a crash "finishing" course in royal etiquette before she accepts her own title—if, indeed, she wants to accept it all.

Mia's makeover from plaid-skirted, bespectacled geek into a glamorous princess is the film's central device, and as such required an actress who could convincingly play both the before and after—not to mention the ungainly "in between" stage.

The actress who landed the role, and stars in its sequel, *Princess Diaries 2*, was then-seventeen-year-old Anne Hathaway, a tall, reed-thin beauty from New York whose biggest previous credit was a regular role on the short-lived Fox series *Get Real* in the fall of 2000. Casting director Ross was impressed with what she saw of Hathaway's talent on that show's pilot, as well as with a general meeting she'd had with the actress the previous spring in New York.

"Sometimes you just have a strong feeling," Ross recalls. "And it's not that we didn't test other people, but there was something about Anne I had a big, big feeling about. That does happen in casting, but not always quite like this."

Ross recounts another early contender's brief run at the role, illustrating the unique balance the part required.

"We got a tape from somebody in Canada early on [who] was very lovely, wonderful," Ross recalls of an actress named Meghan Black (*Elf*). "We had her come in and she tested with Garry. She was really wonderful, a great actress, but we didn't really quite feel that she could make the transition to princess. She was a wonderful actress, but couldn't go from gawky to royal."

If Ross had similar doubts about Hathaway, who was in the running from the early stages, these were assuaged in a slightly unconventional way. This young film princess, it turns out, might thank Fox's publicity department for fast-tracking her to the front of the line for a role at Disney.

"I remember getting this package of publicity stuff from her representation," Ross recalls. "and there were all these amazing pictures, which I guess they'd been taking for various magazines because [*Get Real*] had been on a while, and you see her in all these incredible get-ups." From the actress's demo tape, Ross says, "You could see that she was funny. But with those photos, you could see that she could be made to be very glamorous. She has a certain poise and sophistication that was really innate, that the character just had to get to."

Like her inner and outer qualifications for the glamorous side of the role, Hathaway's comic abilities were as much a matter of physicality as sensibility.

"Anne is a great physical comedienne, and I think that really is the big thing," Ross avers. "She's beautiful and has the ability to transform—she was still young, she was in high school—into the elegant person. But her physical comedy, her talent for that, her instinct for that, really lends itself well to many aspects of the character."

Hathaway's relatively towering height—she's 5'8"—was certainly a big factor in both the character's awkward and stately moments. And while in the screen test Disney did to try her out, she was dressed in the plaid-skirted school uniform look she sports in the first third of the film, she wasn't quite as "geeked out" as she was when we first glimpse her.

"They gave her those eyebrows and all those hair extensions, so they made her look bad," Ross explains of the makeup and hair job done for the film by Hallie D'Amore and Carolyn Elias, respectively.

TO TAPE OR NOT TO TAPE

That's not to say that casting the young would-be star was easy. In fact, between the time she'd initially met with Ross and the time Ross wanted her to read for director Garry Marshall, Hathaway had signed with the William Morris Agency in New York. While Ross and the studio were very interested in her, they did have other possibilities in the mix; they were not in a position to fly her out to L.A. for a reading, and a visit to New York wasn't in the cards. So they requested that Hathaway simply do a reading in New York on video and send the tape to the West Coast. While this is a common practice with bicoastal casting efforts, William Morris had other ideas for their precious new client.

"They were protecting her," Ross says of WMA's decision to refuse to put her on tape. "I think the agents' feeling—and I understand it—is that sometimes, if you see somebody for the first time on tape, [Garry] could have looked at it and, for whatever reason—like, the lighting could have been bad—he would write her off and say no. And I think the agent was right; actors always have a much better chance in the room."

As fraught as they were, the negotiations eventually yielded a test deal that pleased both sides. And then came the casting of the other youth parts, for which Ross and her associates Gail Goldberg and Donna Morong cast a wide net, as must often be done with young actors (see the chapter on *School of Rock*). Various actors read in groups in a series of tests, and among them was Heather Matarazzo for the part of Lily, the school friend of Mia, who provides a much-needed reality check for the budding princess' increasingly alienating transformation into royalty.

Matarazzo, who came to prominence as the bespectacled misanthrope of *Welcome to the Dollhouse* and is also East Coast-based, apparently didn't get paired with Hathaway in those initial round-robin tests. She flew back East without an offer, let alone much interest from director Marshall. But later, when the part of Lily remained stubbornly uncast, Ross went to bat for Matarazzo.

"I loved Heather, and she had been there from the beginning," Ross recalls. "So at that point, I said to Garry, 'I know you didn't respond to Heather, but can you just do me a favor, can we just see her again? You don't have to cast her, but I just have a feeling.'" By this time, Anne Hathaway had been cast as Mia, so she read with Matarazzo, and the match was obvious.

"I don't [think] she read with Anne the first time, because we were mixing and matching all kinds of people together," Ross explains. At their reading together, "They just had great chemistry. That was a perfect example where I was really glad that I said, 'Please, can we just bring her back one more time.' When she read that last time with Anne, when you saw them together, it just worked."

Indeed, there's a moment late in the film when the two are running down a tree-lined sidewalk, and the resemblance to another pair of plucky young urban women is undeniable. (Hint: Their TV theme song included the words, "Schlemiel, schlamazel...")

One has to imagine this was faintly obvious to the director of *The Princess Diaries*. According to Ross, that's not all that Garry Marshall is clued into.

"I have to say about working with Garry—he's cast a million things, going back to all that television," Ross says. "And when you work with Garry, he just *gets* it; you know, you bring people in the room, and he *knows*—he knows what they've got. He sees beyond the obvious. You don't waste a lot of time with him, bringing in zillions of people just to see. You bring in good people, he knows it. And I love that about working with him. He's got a great eye for talent and a great eye for comedy."

Marshall's eye for talent even led him to tweak the script a bit.

"Patrick Flueger was a kid we'd seen on a tape from Minnesota," Ross recounts. He was trying out for the part of Michael, Mia's love interest, but wasn't considered seasoned enough for that. It might also have the "nuclear red" hair dye job he'd given himself the night before the taping in Minnesota.

Whatever it was that caught Ross's eye, she got Marshall to pay attention, too.

"I said to Garry at the time, 'You know, there's something really great about this kid.' He was sixteen, and he'd never acted professionally before; he was in a band and he did theatre in high school."

There was a small part for a quirky schoolmate of Mia's named Boris ("Eastern European, always happy, brainy nerd," reads the Breakdown). Ross says that Marshall had Boris retooled to be "kind of a farm boy"—albeit a farm boy with bright dyed hair, which Flueger kept for the film.

One performer who was interested in the lead role was a celebrity in another medium, pop music. And while the role of Mia wasn't right for this newcomer to acting, there was a role that fit—and which she pulled off with sporting aplomb.

"For Lana, we had met Mandy Moore," says Ross of the teen singing sensation who plays the film's jealous head cheerleader ("beautiful, blonde, great figure," according to the Breakdown), who tries in vain to sabotage Mia's social ascent. "She was interested in the role of Mia. We thought she'd be perfect for Lana, but she came in for Mia, because that was the only part she would read for. Of course, who wouldn't want the lead?"

Among other disqualifiers, "She just was a little too sophisticated already. She's a very sophisticated girl. But Garry really loved her for Lana."

It turned to be a fortunate decision, and not only for the movie's sake.

"It actually worked, because with her schedule—she had movies with MTV, commercials, and her music career—it would have been tough for her to do Mia because she was very, very busy. It turned out to be a very good part for her, because I thought she was absolutely great in the role, and it worked well around her very busy schedule."

For the role of Mia's mom, a free-spirited single mother—the Breakdown describes her as a "Bohemian, sexy artist"—who has encouraged her daughter's academic pursuits, if not her grooming and etiquette, the difficulty was that the role was crucial but not large.

"This was a really, really hard part to cast, because it wasn't a big part but you needed somebody really solid," Ross recalls. "A lot of the people we were really interested in weren't interested in the role, because it was small..."

In the midst of reading other people, Ross received a tape from the English actress Caroline Goodall (a favorite of Steven Spielberg's, with parts in *Schindler's List* and *Hook*).

"I knew Caroline, I had met her before," Ross explains. She popped in the tape, she says, and saw Goodall in character in the fictional kingdom of Genovia (shades of Elijah Wood's career-making tape for *The Lord of the Rings*). Clearly, for such a role, it helps to live in Italy with a seasoned cameraman, Nicola Pecorini. "Her husband's a cinematographer, and they were in Italy at their home, and she did an incredible test, as if she was in this castle in Genovia."

Though one sees glimpses of this mythical land in the first film, *Princess Diaries 2* is largely set in Genovia—a sort of cross between Luxembourg and Monaco, where, as Ross says, "Everyone talks like Julie Andrews."

Which leads to one of the film's most satisfying "inter-textual" ironies: that the part of Mia's regal "Grandmere," who is charged with the girl's makeover from duck to swan, is played by none other than the original Eliza Doolittle herself.

"We did lists [for the part], and we went through it, and she just seemed like the perfect person," Ross says of the casting of Andrews, herself no stranger to the Disney fold.

The *Pygmalion* narrative of the new film not only casts this former Eliza in the position of a disapproving Henry Higgins to her struggling granddaughter, it incidentally also represents a recurring theme for director Garry Marshall, whose *Pretty Woman* recast *My Fair Lady* as the paradoxically innocent tale of a Hollywood hooker transformed into a modern-day princess by a rich john.

OFF SCRIPT

Wendkos' original script, based on Meg Cabot's novella, underwent some changes from its original draft, and some are reflected in the Breakdown. An "African princess" named Tina, whose "classmates consider her a snob because of her regal manner and constant bodyguard," didn't make it into the film. Ostensibly Tina—whose African-American bodyguard "Wahim" was also listed in the initial Breakdown—had been included as a cautionary contrast for Mia's journey; who'd want to be a princess if it singled you out as a pariah?

Another significant change came when Mia's "distant (but loving) father" was killed off. Rather than being the bearer of the unlikely news that his heritage means his estranged daughter is a princess, it is the father's death that brings the news. In the completed film, Mia has a picture of her late father by her bed; as Ross explains, the bearded figure in the photo is Hathaway's actual father.

Many of the film's other parts were filled, Ross says, by director Marshall's "lucky charms"—an informal repertory of actors with whom he regularly works. These would include Hector Elizondo Jr., who plays Mia's taciturn, leather-clad chauffeur/bodyguard, Joe; Larry Miller, who appears in an against-type (and officially uncredited) turn as a mincing, heavily accented European "stylist," and Patrick Richwood, a forlorn-looking character actor who appeared in memorable small parts in Marshall's *Beaches*, *Pretty Woman*, *The Other Sister*, and *Runaway Bride*, who in *Princess Diaries* has the unforgettably peculiar role of Mr. Robutusen, Mia's suburban neighbor, who never seems to leave his front yard, where he stands murmuring lines from the soap operas he supposedly writes for a living.

"Garry uses a lot of the same people in many of his movies," Ross avers. "Garry's very good about giving people opportunities—

you know, a lot of these young people who've done acting work at the Falcon, he'll find roles for them."

Ross refers to the Falcon Theatre, a small, 120-seat theatre in Burbank that stands a stone's throw from the Warner Bros. lot, and not too far from Disney, either. For her part, Ross can't resist raving further about her director, with whom she also worked on the sequel.

"He's such a loyal, wonderful guy," says Ross. "The sets are so happy. We were at the wrap party, and everybody was crying, saying, 'We're so sad to have it be over, because it's the happiest experience I've ever had on a movie set.'"

Of course, as the film's casting director Ross might reasonably take some credit for helping to populate that happy working environment.

BREAKDOWN SERVICES, LTD.
Los Angeles (310) 276-9166   New York (212) 869-2003   Vancouver (604) 943-7100   London (01) 459-2781
BREAKDOWN SERVICES, LTD.
www.breakdownservices.com   The Link: www.submitlink.com

The information contained in this document is the exclusive property of Breakdown Services, Ltd. Any unauthorized reproduction, duplication, copying or use of the information contained herein, without prior written consent of Breakdown Services, Ltd., is strictly prohibited.

(File 0608f05-lk) L C H V OVER	***DEL'D IN LA Fri., June 9, 2000, Vol. 2000, #0609***
(0. 0602f02-lk) L	Producers: Whitney Houston, Debra Martin Chase,
WALT DISNEY PICTURES	Mario Iscovich
"PRINCESS DIARIES"	Director: Garry Marshall
FEATURE FILM	Writer: Gina Wendkos
DRAFT: 5/12/00	Casting Director: Marcia Ross
	Casting Associate: Jacqueline Carlson
	Start Date: 9/13/00
	Location: Los Angeles

WRITTEN SUBMISSIONS ONLY TO: MARCIA ROSS

NOTE: WHEREVER POSSIBLE, PLEASE SUBMIT LEGALLY EMANCIPATED MINORS OR 18 TO PLAY YOUNGER.

[MIA]   15, awkward, vulnerable, not an obvious beauty. Must have comedic timing…LEAD

[LILLY]   15, Mia's best friend, off-beat, brilliant student, possibly a genius…LEAD

[HELEN THERMOPOLIS]   35–40, Mia's mom. Bohemian, sexy artist…LEAD

[PHILLIPE RENALDO]   40–50, Mia's dad. Very dignified and attractive, but incredibly straight-backed and stiff. He's the Prince of Genovia (a European principality)…LEAD

[MICHAEL]   17, Lilly's older brother. He is lost, sullen and sexy. He plays the piano but is not particularly good at it. He and Mia eventually fall in love…LEAD

[TINA]   15, African princess. Her classmates consider her a snob because of her regal manner and constant bodyguard. She tries to be hip but is unsuccessful...CO-STAR

[LANA WEINBURGER]   15, beautiful, blonde, great figure. Most popular girl in high school...CO-STAR

[JOSH RICHTER]   17, Lana's boyfriend, handsome, jock. Most popular boy in high school...CO-STAR

[MR. GIANNI]   40s, Mia's charming and sexy algebra teacher. He has a romantic relationship with Helen...LEAD

[PRINCIPAL GUPTA]   50s, Asian, tough-minded principal at Mia's private school...

[WAHIM]   25-40, Tina's African-American bodyguard...

[BORIS PELKOWSKI]   15, Eastern European, always happy, brainy nerd who dresses the part...

STORYLINE: MIA's life as she knows it undergoes a radical change when she learns from her distant (but loving) father, Phillipe, that he is, unbenownst to her, Artur Christoff Phillipe Gerard Grimaldi Renaldo—Prince of Genovia—making her, as his only heir, the Princess of Genovia. Protesting all the way, Mia undergoes "princess lessons" with her regal, powerful "Grandmere," and faces a difficult choice: to decide upon her 16th birthday if she wants to remain Mia of Tribeca or take up the mantle of Princess of Genovia. Her life is turned upside down when the media gets wind of her identity, and Mia finds her friendships getting a bit topsy turvy as well: she has a falling out with LILLY, wins the fawning approbation of the super popular LANA (and her boyfriend JOSH), discovers a new friend in

the wealthy but down to earth TINA, and ultimately, without knowing it, falls in love—with MICHAEL, Lilly's brother. Finally, faced with her momentous decision, Mia announces her choice to the world, and reveals herself as a confident, self-possessed young woman of uncommon strength and spirit...

"CSI" Assembly Required

CSI

In Hollywood, the name of producer Dick Wolf stands not only for his high-quality signature show, *Law & Order,* and its spinoffs, but for another kind of law and order enforced through his casting department: The high turnover on these so-called "franchise" shows reflects Wolf's oft-stated philosophy that a show's star is its storytelling, not its actors. Whether Wolf plays hardball—as he did in 1996 with two actors on *New York Undercover,* who tried in vain to stage a sit-down strike for sweeter contracts—or simply holds the line on actors' salaries, giving even the most beloved ones little incentive to stay for more than a few seasons, Wolf's franchise model has been increasingly influential in a TV network economy that has shrunk in audience share and income. Though executives at CBS might deny it, their growing *CSI* franchise has been patterned in large part on Wolf's success with *Law & Order.* Its newest spinoff, *CSI: New York,* even went head to head with the *Law & Order* mothership on Wednesday nights in the fall of 2004 and gave it a run for its money, ratings-wise.

The *CSI* juggernaut has been formidable competition from the start. It was the initial foray into network TV for Hollywood mogul

Jerry Bruckheimer, who has since annexed television to his long-established feature film domain. He came into the game in late 1999 backing a new show from writer/producer Anthony Zuiker, also a newcomer to network TV (he'd sold just one film script previously), about a forensics team in high-traffic Las Vegas who solve crimes using sophisticated science and investigative savvy. Its large ensemble may have drawn comparisons to any number of similar shows—from *ER* to *NYPD Blue*—and its often deadpan, all-business treatment of extremely lurid, gruesome cases had some critics and fans comparing it to *The X-Files*. But according to April Webster, who cast the pilot and the first eleven episodes, Zuiker's premise was rare enough to generate a genuine buzz.

"It was very exciting for us working on the pilot of *CSI*, because at that time it was a completely new subject," Webster says from her busy office in Burbank, where she also oversees casting for *Alias* and *Lost*. "People were attracted to it. We had people in who didn't get the parts in the pilot who later ended up doing the show, like Pauley Perrette, who—it turns out—has this incredible fascination with forensics. She had studied it! Now, of course, there are three franchises, but at the time it was something new and interesting."

Zuiker's script had another attribute that made Webster's job a little easier. "In Anthony's script, the characters were very individually drawn," says Webster. "Sometimes with big-cast shows, you have to kind of figure out, 'OK, why is this guy different than that guy?' But with this one, each character really had a story."

That's reflected in the Breakdown drafted in January, 2000, which lists six regular leads, among them "Gil Sheinbaum," an ID supervisor and crime scene investigator described as "a cross between Mr. Rogers and Bill Gates...a touch on the loopy side... cool as a cucumber." The Breakdown was drafted, apparently, before executive producer William Petersen was on board—since, as even the casual *CSI* fan could tell you, Petersen plays Investigator Gil Grissom, and he's got just a little more masculine energy than that description would suggest. Indeed, several of the characters changed from this initial Breakdown, including the young leading man, "Nick Ledee," described as a "blond and ripped, seen sporting a diamond-stud earring and several dragon tattoos," and as "having a passionate affair" with a fellow investigator, "Catherine Bellows," an ex-stripper. A revised Breakdown released in February calls him "Nicky Ledee," and tones down both the bad-boy accoutrements ("sporting dragon arm tattoos" is all that's left) and the love interest ("Everybody loves Nick, including Catherine"). "We had a very hard time casting Nick," Webster concedes. She recalls with bemusement the scene used to read prospective Nicks: "He was like, not quite, 'Yo yo yo,' but more, 'Hey, dude, how you doin'?'" Clean-cut Texan George Eads eventually got the role, by then called Nick Stokes and made over into a more down-home hunk.

It was a close call, though: Eads only became available near the tail end of that year's pilot season. He was contractually bound to a short-lived drama called *Grapevine*, but that show had the good fortune of being on the same network, CBS. This meant, Webster explains, that Eads was "pre-approved"—meaning he'd already been through the grueling process of the network test and therefore wasn't unknown to the network's executives. Essentially, this means that the suits had already signed off on Eads' acceptability on CBS.

Eads did do a *CSI* test for the network, Webster recalls, but there wasn't exactly nail-biting tension in the room: He tested alone, without competition. This is relatively rare, Webster explains. "The networks don't like to not have a choice, but in some situations, if somebody is absolutely so clearly your choice, there are occasions where you bring in that one person and say, 'This is the guy.'" Not that Webster hadn't given CBS choices for Nick: Several actors had previously tested for the part, to no avail.

Far easier to cast was the part of investigator Warrick Brown, described in the original Breakdown as a "smooth-looking brother" with a "good b.s. detector...a playful, upbeat, good-natured fellow who can barely contain his glee." By the revised February Breakdown, though, the description had gotten more complicated: Warrick is listed as a "degenerate sports bettor who lives to be in on the action...[as] street-smart and sharp as they come."

Webster says the part was easy to cast because the talent pool of African-American actors in their late twenties and early thirties is so large. "There are so many terrific black actors around [who are] definitely under-used. I think the final test was Allen Payne, Morris Chestnut, and Gary Dourdan—that's pretty hefty competition." Dourdan got the role as much for his eyes as for the air of mystery and danger about him. It gave the writers somewhere to go with Warrick, Webster says. "Gary is a pretty amazing-looking guy, because he's got those light-colored eyes, but he also brought something else. The writers were able to develop Warrick [more deeply], because Gary's got stuff going on behind the eyes. There was something about Gary's look and style that just said, 'That's it.'"

NOT JUST PRETTY FACES

Another early decision was the casting of Marg Helgenberger as Catherine, the former stripper-turned-investigator. Lists of possibilities were made, but Helgenberger was the only one interviewed. And her casting, Webster feels, somewhat belies the show-is-the-star model. "One of the reasons we were so keen on Marg Helgenberger is that she's someone who the television audience knows extremely well and [they] are happy to welcome her back into their homes," Webster says. "Her character on *China Beach* was so popular...it certainly helped balance out our two main leads by having someone who was a well-known television star.

"And someone, by the way, who brilliantly fit the character. Marg is such a wonderful actress, she can bring that humanity to it, so it wasn't just the 'hi-I'm-a-woman-cop' part that is sometimes written."

The part of the unit's Captain, "Frank Myers," was colorfully described as "a fat-chewing son-of-a-bitch who never did shed his Jersey roots...a gruff, dyspeptic sort, humorless...his armor is virtually impenetrable." His age was listed as "in his mid-50s." The revised Breakdown adds the adjective "jaded" and the characteristics "a Jersey temper and no filter in his mouth." One's mind easily flips through a Rolodex of crusty character types: John Spencer, say, or Raymond Barry. The part eventually went to Paul Guilfoyle, a short New Yorker in his late forties with a face that looks like it's frozen in a perpetual frown. Indeed, his impenetrable deadpan is what won him the part (changed somewhere along the way to "Capt. Jim Brass"). "We had older guys in, all the usual guys, and

Paul probably was maybe his late forties when he started," Webster says. "But what I loved about Paul is that he has that very dry, sardonic New York quality where he doesn't have to be in your face; he shows his contempt with a look, or he shows his opinion just with a gesture. He's that kind of actor."

Guilfoyle's unflappable demeanor made a powerful contrast with Petersen's more hotheaded, excitable investigator. In fact, while there was no romantic chemistry to calculate for the original ensemble cast (the Nick-Catherine affair was dropped before shooting began), there was a sort of ensemble chemistry that was important to the producers. Webster says that the tone was set from the top—by CBS head Les Moonves, in fact.

"He had a very specific idea conceptually of what he wanted— he didn't want them to be 'pretty' people," Webster recalls. "He wanted them to be attractive, but he didn't want it to look like, you know, *Baywatch*—nothing against *Baywatch*—but he didn't want just pretty people, he wanted people who had some stuff." And, of course, he wanted this substance to add up to a distinctive recipe, not a cookie-cutter large-cast show. The actors' backgrounds, Webster says, helped in this area. "You know, Petersen is a theatre actor as well as a film actor, and he has very strong connections that way, so the people we were trying to get in there were people who were familiar with that kind of ensemble playing," Webster says. "Because you don't want a diva; you want people who work as a group, as a unit."

RUNNING WITH WOLF

Which brings us, unavoidably, to the one off-screen fracas recently experienced by this otherwise happy family. Last summer the young leads George Eads and Jorja Fox, in the part of Sara Sidle—a role created after the pilot and cast after the show was ordered—were fired from the show for about a week when they reportedly threatened not to show up for work. They were hired back after apparently agreeing to stay at their $100,000-per-episode deals, while claiming that the whole work stoppage threat was a "misunderstanding."

It seemed like a classic test case of the Dick Wolf theory—or an illustration of the joke John Levey tells about the show he has cast and recast since its inception: "*ER* stands for 'everyone's replaceable.'" Webster says she understands the economic pressures that can give ensemble shows trouble—and she insists that such considerations can't enter into the original casting process.

"You can't anticipate what's going to happen when the 'terrible twos' come," Webster says, referring to the growing pains that happen when a show becomes a ratings phenomenon. "And I think whenever there's an inequity with the salaries, people begin to feel like they want to be part of the franchise. But you never cast it that way, anticipating what they'll do. It would be sort of like a pre-nup to do it like that—like you're anticipating the breakup.

"In terms of setting a precedent, when Dick Wolf just replaced those guys on *Street Justice*, he wanted to show that it didn't run on those actors," Webster says. "That happened again with *Law & Order*; he just replaced people. That created the pattern. I think a lot of people felt that when NBC paid the cast of *Friends* all that money, it set a bad precedent. But it's worth it to the studio, and it's worth it to the network, because the money's coming from those shows. If you know have a surefire win, what are you gonna do? You're going to keep that person there as much as you possibly can."

Webster explains, though, how ensemble shows can be at a disadvantage in terms of holding on to their most popular actors. "What happens sometimes when you do a pilot, and it's a good pilot, is that you get people to work on something and maybe not for their usual quote," Webster says. "And then when the pilot goes, you have such a big cast that you can't afford to pay them more. So you sometimes have to recast, or just know that because you're keeping them working, maybe that will take away some of the pain. But, look, to ask actors to work for less money is not our goal, by any means."

There was one bit of recasting from the pilot: The part of "Holly Gribbs," a newbie investigator who gets shot in the first episode but is nonetheless listed as a series regular. The character was played by Chandra West, but somewhere along the way it was decided that Holly Gribbs would not be long for the world of *CSI*.

"She was fatally shot," Webster says of the script change. "And everybody mourns her. Then Jorja Fox came in as a former student who had been mentored by Bill's character." Ironically, Fox was freed up to work on *CSI* when her popular Secret Service agent character on *The West Wing* was written out of the show—not with a bullet, as one might assume, but simply with a flick of Aaron Sorkin's mighty pen. ("I just kind of disappeared into thin air," Fox has said of her *West Wing* exit.)

TAP-DANCING IN THE MIDDLE

Diplomacy and mediation are among the skills required by the work of a television casting director, particularly on a pilot. A casting director is hired by the production company that's making the show, but ultimately the producers must defer in all matters— including casting—to the network or the network/studio that will air the show.

"You're trying to satisfy everybody; that's the casting director's job, to make sure that you're doing everything you can to cover all the bases," Webster explains. "What's going to work for the network, what's going to work for your producers and serve the show? We have to sort of tap-dance in the middle, because we know what's gonna work and what's not gonna work, what may fly and may not fly."

Luckily, in the case of *CSI*, the casting executives at CBS, Lucy Cavallo and Peter Golden, were "amazing throughout the process, really, really helpful," Webster says. Indeed, the support of a network casting department can make all the difference. "Anyone who gets into an adversarial situation with the network is stupid, because they're your best advocates, and they'll help in any way they can," Webster says. "If you make it a collaboration, then you have everyone working toward the same goal, as opposed to against each other. It's really important for the casting director to be that liaison, so it doesn't become, like, 'Network wants this,' or 'The studio wants this,' so they go, 'Well, screw the studio!' Everybody is so sensitive around new material that it can easily go that way.

"The casting director's job isn't simply bringing actors in; it really is about, how do you liaison between the needs of the network and the studio, and the needs of your producers, and make sure that all the needs get met, while also exercising in your creative input?"

That's a lot of balls in the air, but Webster—a seasoned profession-al who's worked with some of the most original writer/producers in television—seems to be a skilled juggler. She cast J.J. Abrams' new hit show *Lost*, she recalls, in a whirlwind of changing scripts, mor-phing characters, and intense industry buzz. But she can also stay focused for the long haul: Two of *CSI*'s regular cast members, Eric Szmanda and Robert David Hall, weren't cast in the pilot but were, as she put it, "favorites of [her] office." Indeed, Webster seems to be able adapt her process to the particular needs of a given project.

"As long as you have is as long as it will take," she says with a philosophical smile. "If you have two weeks to cast it, you'll find your whole cast in two weeks. If you have eight weeks to cast it, you'll find your whole cast in eight weeks. Nobody likes to think that there may be one more name out there.

"With all the best casting directors, no stone goes unturned. We all have this thing—if we see somebody on a show who we don't know, we're like, 'Who is that? How come I don't know him?' It can be the waiter in a movie."

This tirelessness also applies to the standard for which the best casting directors aim. "Everyone wants their cast to be special," Webster says. "That's what you hope for, that magic thing. I don't think anyone goes into casting saying, 'This will be the "okay" cast,' or 'That's "good enough."' You want someone who people will tune in to watch for however many years."

That is, of course, if the actors you painstakingly choose stick around for "however many years." So far, though, it must be said that the biggest difference between *Law & Order* and *CSI* is that the latter franchise has not become a revolving-door clearinghouse of actors.

Some credit for that surely belongs to Webster and her original ensemble assembly.

(File 0215p03-iam) L
(0. 0214p03-ia)
TOUCHSTONE TELEVISION
"C.S.I."
1 HOUR PILOT / CBS
DRAFT: 1/18/00

DEL'D IN LA Wed., Feb. 16, 2000, Vol. 2000, #0216
Exec. Producers: Jerry Bruckheimer
Co-Exec. Producer: Anthony Zuiker
Producers: Jonathan Littman, William Petersen,
    Cindy Chvatal
Writer: Anthony E. Zuiker
Director: TBA
Casting Director: April Webster
Casting Associate: Elizabeth Greenberg
Start Date: 3/2000
Location: L.A.

WRITTEN SUBMISSIONS ONLY TO: APRIL WEBSTER CASTING

[CATHERINE BELLOWS] Mid 30s, is an ex-stripper turned CSI. A single mother of two daughters, ages 3 and 5. Catherine finds herself working the graveyard shift in a male dominated arena. Also, since she's the most senior woman in the department, Catherine is often asked to work the sexual assault cases on children. A tough job for a mother of two...SERIES REGULAR

[NICKY LEDEE] Late 20s, is a stud out of Lincoln, Nebraska. He's a guy's guy. Sporting dragon arm tattoos, a killer smile and an infectious way with people. Everybody loves Nick, including Catherine...SERIES REGULAR

[WARRICK BROWN] Late 20s, is an African-American degenerate sports bettor who lives to be in the action. Warrick's interesting for two reasons. A) He is not a big fan of "guilty" white people. B) He makes more money betting on sports than he does being a CSI. Why? He's street smart and sharp as they come...SERIES REGULAR

[HOLLY GRIBBS]   Mid 20s, is fresh out of the Academy. Juiced by her mother, a Lieutenant in Traffic, Holly finds herself at odds with her new job before she even clocks in. One look at her and we know she's destined for disaster. Indeed, giving a girl like that a CSI job is like asking an alcoholic to tend bar...SERIES REGULAR

[CAPTAIN FRANK MYERS]   Mid 50s, is a jaded son-of-a-bitch who's been stuck in Criminalistics far too long. He's got a Jersey temper and no filter in his mouth. His mission in life is to be promoted to Deputy Chief and make the lives of his investigators miserable...SERIES REGULAR

GIL SHEINBAUM: CAST (WILLIAM PETERSEN)

STORYLINE: Crime Scene Investigators are young forensic specialists who solve crimes on the most unpredictable shift in America. Graveyard in Las Vegas. In a sleepless city that hosts a million tourists a month, crime is rampant. Hence, CSI's have a tough job. They must rely on smarts, science, and good old-fashioned gut to restore peace of mind to their victims...

A Dream Team on a Wishful "Wing"

The West Wing

Truth is stranger than fiction, goes the old saying. But what axiom would apply to the increasingly unreal alternate universe of NBC's award-bedecked drama *The West Wing*?

In the years since the series about a fictional Democratic president's White House staff debuted in 1999, the nation's highest office has changed hands, and political priorities, more dramatically than even a quick-cut reality TV show could keep up with. In just five years, the real world of American politics—from the contested 2000 presidential election to the 2001 terrorist attacks and their complicated geopolitical aftermath—has surpassed the imagination of even the most apocalyptic fabulist.

But then, headline-ripping relevance was never the intention of *The West Wing*, even if the fictional presidency of Josiah "Jed" Bartlet happened to hit the airwaves during a real-life Democratic presidency. The conception, as John Levey, the pilot's co-casting director explained, was more timeless than that.

"We were very much charged with the responsibility, by [creator] Aaron [Sorkin] particularly, but by [producer] John [Wells] and [director] Tommy [Schlamme], as well, that this was to be the government we wish we had," says Levey, who collaborated with his longtime *ER* colleague Kevin Scott to populate the bustling ensemble cast of *The West Wing*. "This was to be the best and the brightest. If the nation were in these people's hands, we would all feel good."

That mandate ended up influencing the casting in a number of ways—from the hiring of an iconic American actor, Martin Sheen, as much known for his offscreen liberal activism as for his acting work, to the preference for seasoned, often stage-trained actors to round out the cast.

As Levey explains of the latter: "It couldn't just be great-looking people in their 20s, because how the hell did they get there? Tommy [Schlamme] was always saying, 'It's not enough just to put glasses on and pretend someone is smart. They have to *be* smart.' [They have] to walk the walk and talk the talk."

Talk indeed: Sorkin's writing, particularly for the series *Sports Night* and for *The West Wing*, is dense and crackling, suggesting a cross between the rapid-fire dialogue of Preston Sturges comedies and the offhanded, fly-on-the-wall realism of Robert Altman. And, given the series' setting, the show's dialogue is typically a jargon-packed game of insider baseball with huge, life-or-death stakes.

"It's not kitchen drama, where you're just saying, 'I love you,' or, 'Mom, can I have the keys?'" Levey avers. "It's about words and concepts and ideas that most of us don't understand."

Lending his character's ideas some flesh-and-blood substance is Sheen, whose off-screen political causes have included no-nukes, homeless advocacy, and migrant workers, among others, and who made headlines when he was named honorary mayor of his home-town of Malibu—then promptly decreed it "a nuclear-free zone, a sanctuary for aliens and the homeless, and a protected environment for all life, wild and tame." In the original Breakdown, published November 16, 1998, President Bartlet isn't described as a left-wing activist per se, but he's clearly somewhat idealized: He's a New Hampshire native descended from one of the signers of the Declaration of Independence, and he's central enough a character to merit a direct quote, apparently from Sorkin's pilot script, that stands out in the midst of Levey and Scott's Breakdown summary:

"Looking every bit the country lawyer, you wouldn't immediately guess that he's brilliant, which he is. While the left hand is lulling you with folksy charm, you don't even hear the right hook coming."

Remarkably, as much as that folksy-like-a-fox personality, embodied so definitively by Sheen, is the series' moral center and compass, President Bartlet was originally conceived only as a "recurring character," a background figure to the foregrounded stories of his busy, competitive staff.

Tested early on for the part were Bob Gunton, who had toured in a solo show as FDR but is best known to moviegoers as the warden in *The Shawshank Redemption*, and John Cullum, who became familiar for his regular role on *Northern Exposure* and, as Levey recalls, had just finished a multi-episode arc playing Anthony Edwards' father on *ER*. Neither, however, is a household name, and as such would have fit the show's original conception, Levey says.

"Everybody essentially agreed that they were wonderful actors," Levey recalls, "and that if it was going to be about the staff and the president was going to be secondary, they would be all right."

But when Sheen entered the casting process—apparently some time before the first Breakdown came out, since it lists Bartlet as a "series regular"—the balance of star power changed.

"As Martin became available, suddenly we thought, What would be the point of having Martin Sheen if you can't use him every week? Martin's so Kennedy-esque," Levey continues. "He brings gravitas."

That may be because, while he's further to the left than President Bartlet, political commitment isn't something Sheen has to fake.

"I remember that Martin early on called to say that he might not be able to be at work on Monday," Levey recalls. "And you know, you're always suspicious—actor's reasons for that are often rather personal, and rather vain, and not terribly important. And when asked, Martin said he was going to the San Onofre nuclear power plant to demonstrate, and that he might get arrested on Sunday, and he might not be able to get back on Monday morning, and he could maybe make a late afternoon work call, because he was sure he could make his bail. That's a whole different thing than being drunk in Vegas.

"Martin's principles are wonderful, even if you don't agree with his policy views. He's a devoutly religious Catholic—I mean, he *is* Kennedy-esque, in more ways than his visage. It's in his being; morality is a huge part of how he makes decisions."

Sheen also has gifts that might be considered presidential.

"He also is very much like a politician in the best sense," Levey says. "When my mom was sick, he heard about it. He had met her once, and when I next saw him, he called her Sylvia and asked how she was, in that way politicans do. It's like, How the hell do you remember my mother?"

As a veteran casting professional, Levey knows one of the central truths of casting, particularly in this media-saturated age.

"Certainly actors bring their whole careers—and nowadays, because of [the press], they bring their whole personal lives—into every part. You can't not know Sean Penn's personal stories, and it impacts how you feel about his work. In Martin's case, what people know about him gives the presidency moral authority."

Adds Levey, in an oblique swipe at the real West Wing's current occupant, "Not reproducing life as it is today, of course."

TEST BAN

Different associations would attach to *The West Wing*'s other "name" actor, Rob Lowe, who would play Deputy Communications Director Sam Seaborn, described in the Breakdown as a "strictly political animal" who's "not the most well-read guy in the world," and whose B storyline in the pilot involved a minor peccadillo with a "part-time hooker."

Casting film star Lowe was more than just a matter of bringing in "a lot of tune-in for the first episode," as Levey puts it.

"That was in some ways the most interesting piece of casting," Levey recalls. "Rob came in as well prepared and as interested in the role and as right for the role as anybody could possibly have been. He hit a gigantic home run."

He may in fact have been almost too good for the part—at least, that's what Lowe's representatives seemed to think.

"His people took the position, 'That's it, you've seen it once, we're not going to test him,'" Levey recounts. "And that got the backs up of the studio people, the network people, involved with the production."

That bit of agency hardball sent the casting directors scrambling for a Plan B: Perhaps Bradley Whitford, whom they had in mind for the show's other youngish lead role, Deputy Chief of Staff Joshua Lyman, could play Sam, and they would find another Josh. Or perhaps they could just find a new Sam, at least as a way to force Lowe's hand.

"We spent quite a lot of time moving Brad to Sam and trying to find a new Josh, moving Brad back to Josh and trying to find another Sam, for the whole duration of the process," Levey recalls. "A very short time before shooting, a deal was made with Rob. That set of events is related to events that happened years later, in terms of deals and departures."

Levey refers, of course, to Lowe's leaving the series after three seasons. While the reason Lowe gave the press at the time was that "it has been increasingly clear... there was no longer a place for Sam Seaborn on *The West Wing*," there was surely something to reports of dissatisfaction with his salary deal. Lowe, it was reported, wanted but hadn't received a raise from $75,000 an episode; Sheen's salary, meanwhile, had been upped to $300,000 per show.

Far less difficult was filling the role of Leo McGarry, the president's Chief of Staff, named "Leo Jacobi" on the original Breakdown, which goes on to describe him as "fifty-five-years-old and professorial...with a dryly sarcastic sense of humor," "a stickler when it comes to crossword puzzles" who thinks his boss is "a klutz and a spaz."

"At John Wells Productions, we had just cast a television show called *Trinity*, where John Spencer had played the father of the Irish Catholic family," Levey recalls. The crusty but sympathetic Spencer had a long resumé in roles as police chiefs, generals, dads, and uncles, and he brings his own brand of authority, seasoned with an authentic working-class grit, to the role. "I believe he was the only person we read for Leo," Levey says. "His audition was spectacular. That was the first piece that fell in."

Whitford was apparently an actor that creator Sorkin had brought into the process, and apart from the contention over which role he'd play, Sam or Josh, he was a relatively easy choice. The other two major characters, Communications Director Toby Ziegler and White House Press Secretary C.J. Gregg, each came down to strong either/or choices at the network test level.

"Richard Schiff did an outstanding reading [for Toby], but he also tested against Eugene Levy," Levey says. Schiff certainly fit the Breakdown's description of a "rumpled and sleepless" worrier with "a cynical sense of of humor."

But former *SCTV* comic Eugene Levy's test was also a strong contender, Levey recalls.

"I'd say that in all the years I've been casting, Eugene's reading was the best reading of someone who didn't get the job. In fact, in some ways, just for that narrow experience of the audition itself, he maybe did a better reading than Richard. But we had worked with Richard on *ER*, and we knew his work very well, and we felt that there would be a wider palette to draw on in the long run. That was maybe the hardest decision. Well, that and C.J."

Described in the Breakdown as "quite coolly competent," C.J. is a key mediator between warring factions in the pilot script, as well as the brave public face of the White House. She is also described as "compact and athletic," which is about half right for the two very different actresses who made it to the final round of casting: CCH Pounder and Allison Janney.

Auditioning actors, take note: according to Levey, "All that physical stuff we provide in those descriptions doesn't mean a goddamn thing," Levey explains.

Adds co-casting director Kevin Scott, "When someone like Allison or CC comes in and reads, you can forget about all that physicality, you know?"

And so two physically imposing women tested opposite each other for C.J., and, as with the role of Toby, it was a photo finish.

"In many ways going into the audition, everybody hoped it would be CCH, partly because of the race issue, also because of how fabulous she is," Levey says. "But Allison was funnier, and ultimately more unique for television. She had something."

Turning to his colleague, Levey adds, "I didn't really know Allison before we began the process, did you?"

"Yes, I did," says Scott. "I don't know if you knew this, but I held her hand through the process. She was a nervous wreck; I don't think she had ever gone through this process before. I felt bad, because I know CC well, but I also knew Allison needed some special attention. CC had been through this a hundred times."

"And you were still green enough to be nurturing," Levey jokes.

Scott's attention paid off. And, as he recalls, he got some unexpected feedback from the show's star.

"I'm in the middle of a whole bunch of people for an upcoming episode and I hear all this commotion," Scott recounts. "[Martin's] sitting outside in the waiting area with all the actors, and they're all excited, because they're like, 'Oh my God, I'm going to be reading with Martin!' Martin comes in, interrupts me in the middle of the audition, and goes, 'Hey, what's up, Kevin?' And he sits down. And I'm thinking, OK, I've got twenty people out there, and I'm way behind. And he goes, 'I've just got one question for you. Where'd you find that scene-stealing bitch?'"

As Scott tells it, there was an awkward pause before the gotcha.

"I didn't know how to respond. And then he was like, 'I'm just joking! She's fabulous! Where'd you guys find her?' It was hilarious. You know, he's like that."

Indeed, it was Janney's first experience with the notorious network test—that fraught, high-pressure final callback in front of not only the show's writers and producers but for the studio and network executives, as well. Levey explains that John Wells—executive producer of *ER* as well as *The West Wing* and *Third Watch*—tries his best to humanize this nerve-wracking process.

"John is unique," Levey explains. "I don't know what other producers do, but he brings all of the people who are testing for a show together, and he says, 'You're all here because we like all of you. We don't know who we want. We don't have a favorite. We're open to see what happens in the process. We thank you. We know that this is barbaric, it's impossible, but no one's ever been able to figure out a better way to do it.' He's so nurturing and reassuring.

"Because when you think about it, especially when it's a young people's pilot, half of the kids who are testing made under $25,000 the year before, and if they get the job and it goes to series, which are both long shots, they'll be making $20 grand an episode. It's a $450,000 audition, and often the auditions are under five minutes. On a social or personal or professional level, if you had five minutes to establish your value of a quarter of a million or half a million dollars—it's very difficult."

CALL THE SORKIN MAN

The *West Wing* audition process had at least one other uncommon feature that set it apart from business as usual, according to Scott.

"One of the things that was unique about the pilot of *West Wing* was that often Aaron [Sorkin] read, rather than the casting people," Scott recalls of the auditions. "He just loves to read opposite actors. For one thing, he reads faster than any human being could ever speak. We used to joke, it was like watching the Chinese national ping-pong tournament: You can't tell the difference between a lob and a slam unless you're trying to send it back. Aaron's ball moves really fast. And if you can't keep up yourself, then you can't really tell how the actor's doing."

Indeed, as mentioned before, actors who can't jump through the verbal hoops of Sorkin's writing need not apply.

"There are a lot of really great people who can't do *West Wing*," explains Levey, "because language is not their skill base."

"Someone who's believable as a police officer is probably not believable as a policy writer," Scott elaborates. But he makes a quick exception for one actor who's played roles all up and down the class ladder: "[John] Spencer can flip around in so many different arenas, because he's a character man."

Casting the pilot involved more than just finding the six leads (there was actually a seventh series regular, a political consultant and love interest for Josh played by Moira Kelly, who ended up lasting just fourteen of the first season's twenty-one episodes because her storyline didn't pan out). There were also nine other "possible recurring roles" listed, as well as three small guest parts particular to the pilot's plot. As with their work in staffing the bustling hospital of *ER*, Levey and Scott worked to fill in the background as well as the foreground of the fictional Bartlet administration.

"It was very much like the *ER* pilot in the sense that there were the leads who were the doctors, and then there were all these nurses and desk clerks and physicians—you were setting up a gigantic trampoline for the stars to jump on, and the rest of those people were part of it," Levey explains.

In the case of *The West Wing*, the equivalent of nurses and desk clerks were such roles as Donnatella Moss, Josh's young assistant, played by Janel Moloney; Sam's secretary Cathy, described in the Breakdown as Asian-American, and played for two seasons by Suzy Nakamura; reporter Billy, a character who didn't recur past the pilot, played by Marc Grapey; Mallory, the schoolteacher daughter of Leo McGarry, played by Allison Smith; Margaret, Leo's secretary, played by NiCole Robinson; Leo's wife, who didn't end up appearing until the fourth episode, played by Sara Botsford (who didn't recur after that); the popular Mrs. Landingham, the president's private secretary, memorably played by Kathy Joosten, and two parts that didn't even make it into the pilot, let alone recur: an assistant for Moira Kelly's character and a young aide for President Bartlet.

Longtime followers of the series may be baffled by this lineup, since so many other regular and recurring characters have come and gone, from President Bartlet's strong-willed First Lady, played by Stockard Channing, to his Vice President, played by Tim Matheson. While these characters may have been in Sorkin's plans for the series—indeed, according to Levey, the reporter later played by Timothy Busfield was in the works early on—they weren't in the pilot.

One of these series mainstays, added by episode three, was Bartlet's aide Charlie Young—a vestige of that young aide from the original Breakdown who didn't appear in the pilot. The character was reintroduced into the show in part because of a public outcry in the fall of 1999 over the networks' fall lineups, none of which featured minorities, particularly African-Americans, among their regular casts. The NAACP even went so far as to threaten a boycott, and networks responded by hastily retooling their ensembles.

As Scott and Levey recall, Sorkin at first thumbed his nose at this top-down tinkering—not out of racial animosity but out of artistic feistiness.

"I remember when they first asked Aaron to write a strong and important African-American part, he made the president's doctor African-American—and then killed him off in a plane crash in the next episode," Levey recalls with a laugh. "It was kind of like, 'Don't tell me what to do.'"

Actually, it was the episode in which the President learns of his physician's untimely death that Dulé Hill made his debut as Charlie. It was Scott, himself an African-American, who introduced the handsome young actor into the mix. Levey calls it "one of the best pieces of casting that was done on *West Wing*."

As Levey recalls, "The network was under pressure, and put us under some pressure to add an African-American character. And Kevin brought Dulé to everybody's attention, and Dulé, in more ways than racially, is a unique part of the show. He's such a dignified character."

Sheen, it turns out, is not the only member of *The West Wing* team with real-life political interests.

"My mother used to be chief of staff for Congressman Ron Dellums," Scott says, referring to the black legislator from his native Bay Area, who was the highest-ranking African-American in Congress for decades. "He was in Congress for damn near thirty years, and at one point he was chairman of the Armed Services Committee. And my aunt, Barbara [Lee], took his seat after he retired."

Scott's mother, Carlottia Scott, also worked for years as chief of politics for the Democratic National Committee. These family connections didn't just give Scott insights into the world of politics—they had something to do with the reason the series earned a fan in high places.

"President Clinton sent us both congratulatory personal letters at the time that we won our Emmys," Levey recounts. "It was like, 'Carlottia's boy got the Emmy!' The Clinton White House—they watched *The West Wing*.

"I don't think Bush does. His people don't seem to be as interested."

 Los Angeles   New York   Vancouver   London
(310) 276-9166   (212) 869-2003   (604) 943-7100   (01) 459-2781

BREAKDOWN SERVICES, LTD.
www.breakdownservices.com   The Link: www.submitlink.com

(File: 1113p01-kf) L N	***DEL'D IN LA Mon., Nov. 16, 1998, Vol. 1998, #1116***
(O. 1112p02-rh)	Executive Producers: John Wells, Aaron Sorkin
JOHN WELLS PRODUCTIONS/	Producer: Kristin Harms
WBTV	Director: TBA
"THE WEST WING"	Writers: Aaron Sorkin
PILOT/NBC	Sr. V.P. of Talent: Barbra Miller
DRAFT: 2/6/98	Casting Directors: John Levey/ Kevin Scott
	Sr. Casting Coordinator: Cheryl Kloner
	Casting Coordinator: Maxine Harris
	Starting Date: Approx. 2/1/99
	Location: Pilot TBD; Serious L.A.

WRITTEN SUBMISSION ONLY TO: JOHN LEVEY/ KEVIN SCOTT

SCRIPTS AVAILABLE: 11/18

NOTE: DIRECT ALL SUBMISSIONS AND INQUIRIES TO KEVIN SCOTT'S OFFFICE.

DUPLICATE SUBMISSIONS (COVER LETTERS ONLY) TO BARBRA MILLER AT THE ABOVE ADDRESS.

[SAM SEABORN]   Early 30s, Sam is the Deputy Communications Director at the White House. The subordinate to Toby Ziegler, Sam works closely with Leo, Josh, Toby, and C.J., planning an appropriately Presidential response to the events of the day. Not the most well-read guy in the world, Sam works in the White House, but is a strictly political animal—he knows nothing of the history of the White House, and is under the mistaken impression that FDR was the 16th President of the United States. While the rest of the staff wrestles with the main event of the day (the President's broken ankle, the Cuban refugees headed towards Florida, and Joshua's major gaffe on yesterday's *Meet the Press*), Sam deals with a little personal problem all his own. The women he met and went to bed with last night is not just cheerful and attractive to him—she's also a part-time hooker, and that kind of faux pas that can ruin an ambitious man's career for good... SERIES REGULAR (1)

[JOSHUA LYMAN]   A youthful man in his 30s, Josh is the Deputy Chief of Staff, working directly beneath Leo Jacobi, and is highly regarded as a brain. Josh helped elect President Bartlet; during the campaign, he had an affair with gifted political consultant Mandy Hampton. He broke up with Mandy after he was tapped to go to the White House and she was let go, but he's clearly still very much attracted to her. A very liberal Democrat who has nothing but contempt for the Religious Right, Josh is in the doghouse after a disastrous appearance on *Meet the Press*, during which he smugly denounced Mary Marshy, a spokesperson for Christian Family Values. Believed to be on the verge of losing his job, Josh is on tenterhooks throughout the day, and even agrees to apologize to Mary Marsh for his thoughtless sarcasm. Delighted to learn that Mandy is back in town (and not so delighted to find she's working for the opposition), Josh gets a surprise when the President shows up unexpectedly to back him during a conference with Mary Marsh and Reverend Al Caldwell... SERIES REGULAR (8)

[TOBY ZIEGLER]   In his 40s, a rumpled and sleepless Communications Director at the White House, Toby is Sam's boss, and he works closely on a day-to-day basis with Leo, Sam, and C.J. A man with a cynical sense of humor, Toby worries about the political implications of every decision, and is peeved with Josh for his uncalled-for remarks on *Meet the Press*. After raking Josh over the coals for having vastly exceeded the parameters for his instructions, Toby tries to preserve Josh's job by arranging a peace meeting. But when Toby attends the pow-wow with Mary Marsh and Reverend Caldwell, he blows his own stack when he thinks Mary is making anti-Semitic cracks about Josh himself... SERIES REGULAR (13)

[MADELINE "MANDY" HAMPTON]   An attractive and instantly likeably woman in her mid to late 30s, Mandy is a top political consultant, who had an affair with Josh during Bartlet's presidential campaign. Intelligent and ambitious but sometimes a bit scattered, Mandy did not go to the White House along with everyone else; Josh got tapped for his slot, and Mandy went off to a $650,000 per year consulting job. However, Mandy has just returned to Washington with a new job—as political consultant for her lover, Senator Lloyd Russell. Intrigued to be back in the same town with Josh, Mandy intends to stage-manage Russell's bid for the presidency, and hopes to be fighting toe-to-toe against Josh all the way. Quite pleased to have lunch with Josh, she lets him know that their new relationship will be personally friendly but professionally adversarial… SERIES REGULAR (3)

[LEO JACOBI]   55 years old and professorial, Leo is the President's Chief of Staff. A stickler when it comes to his crossword puzzles, Leo knows President Bartlet quite well—and regards him as a klutz and a spaz. Leo is furious with Josh for his *Meet the Press* debacle; he chews Josh out royally, but appears to have no intention for firing him. None too thrilled with the lack of solid intelligence about the Cuban refugees, Leo clearly keeps careful watch on the pulse of the nation, despite the fact that no two economists can agree on anything. A man with a dryly sarcastic sense of humor, he hits the ground running when Josh brings him evidence that Senator Lloyd Russell is running for president against Bartlet…SERIES REGULAR (2) PLEASE SUBMIT ACTORS OF ALL RACES AND ETHNICITES.

[C.J. GREGG]   In her early 30s, compact, athletic, and quite coolly competent, C.J. lives in Georgetown and is the White House Press Secretary. Used to working closely with Toby and Joshua, C.J. is in charge of briefing the press, conducting press conferences, and deflecting their awkward questions with grace and skill. She spends

most of her day evading questions about Josh's gaffe, and fears that the press are bloodhounds on his scent. She tries to moderate the tempers during the conference with Caldwell and his supporters… SERIES REGULAR (3) PLEASE SUBMIT ACTORS OF ALL RACES AND ETHNICITIES.

[PRESIDENT JOSIAH (JED) BARTLET]   The President of the United States, Bartlet is a Democrat from New Hampshire, and is descendant of one of the original signers of the Declaration of Independence. "Looking every bit the country lawyer, you wouldn't immediately guess that he's brilliant, which he is. While the left hand is lulling you with folksy charm, you never see the right hook coming." Regarded by his staff (especially Leo) as a klutz, Bartlet has just added to his reputation by riding a bicycle into a tree and spraining his ankle. When he returns to the White House, he reveals why: he was in a rage because an anti-abortion movement called Lambs of Christ sent his thirteen-year-old daughter a Raggedy Ann doll with a knife stuck in its throat. Still furious but under control, he wastes no time kicking Reverend Al Caldwell out of the White House and ordering him to denounce the LoC publicly. He demands that his staff re-focus their attention on the real problem: the Cuban refugees… SERIES REGULAR (60)]

[DONNATELLA MOSS]   Josh's assistant, known as Donna, she is 25 and sexy without trying too hard. She is devoted to Josh, but resolutely refuses to bring him coffee—until today, when she's half-certain Josh is going to be fired. She's been his assistant for two and a half years, and believes that Josh has instrumental in winning the election for President Bartlet. She later shows concern for the President's daughter, who has received a particularly memorable piece of hate mail… 20 lines, 4 scenes (7) POSSIBLE RECURRING ROLE

[CATHY]   A pretty Asian-American woman, Cathy is Sam's secretary, a very competent woman who keeps Sam's head screwed on a little straighter. She gives Sam the bad news that he must give a tour of the White House to a group of fourth-graders, and is mildly appalled by Sam's desperate efforts to evade the responsibility… 1 speech & 16 lines, 5 scenes (36) POSSIBLE RECURRING ROLE

[DAISY REESE]   Mandy's assistant, Daisy is a chain-smoking 25-year-old super-brain. Quite furious that her boss has totally screwed up the details of their move to new offices in Washington, Daisy is convinced that she's going to spend countless fruitless hours sorting through cartons, all because Mandy misplaced the guide to the boxes' contents. Sarcastic and needling, Daisy doesn't try for an instant to hide her disdain for Mandy's mistake… 1 speech and 14 lines, 1 scene (30) POSSIBLE RECURRING ROLE

[BILLY]   A well-known Washington reporter, Billy is a hard-working member of the press corps, who tries hard to get Sam to give him a statement about Joshua Lyman's future. Convinced by Sam's stonewalling that Josh is on his way out the door, Billy spreads that rumor far and wide among the members of the working press… 11 lines, 3 scenes (1) POSSIBLE RECURRING ROLE

[MALLORY O'BRIAN]   A young fourth grade teacher, she brings her students to the White House, and is given a guided tour by Sam Seaborn. When it's clear that Sam is utterly ignorant about the history of this most famous building, she takes him aside for a dressing-down, and is none too impressed with his lame defense. She reveals to him, with some irritation, that she is the daughter of Leo Jacobi, and clearly regards him as a moron… 3 speeches & 13 lines, 2 scenes (51) POSSIBLE RECURRING ROLE

[MARGARET]   Leo's secretary, Margaret isn't sure if Leo's dictated letter to the *New York Times* is for real, and later brings President Bartlet a note . . . 1 line, 2 scenes (12) POSSIBLE RECURRING ROLE

[MRS. JACOBI]   The wife of Leo Jacobi, and the mother of Mallory O'Brian, she tells Sam when "POTUS" is calling for him. She still holds a grudge against Sam because he made a pass at her once, not knowing she was Leo's wife... 2 lines, 1 scene (3)) POSSIBLE RECURRING ROLE

[MRS. LANDINGHAM]   The President's private secretary, she worriedly asks Leo about the President's health, and lets him know she doesn't appreciate flippant chat about the President's physical awkwardness... 5 lines, 1 scene (11) POSSIBLE RECURRING ROLE

[CHARLIE]   19-years-old and fresh-faced in a Brooks Brothers suit, Charlie is taking a year off from Georgetown to work as the President's personal aide. He carries Bartlet's duffel bag and briefcase when he returns to the White House... no lines, 1 scene (60)) POSSIBLE RECURRING ROLE

[LAURIE]   An attractive woman at a hotel bar, she checks Sam out, and later goes to bed with him. A devotee of pot, Laurie smokes furiously after sex, and is miffed (maybe a little hurt) when Sam excuses himself to go to work at 5:30 in the morning. Unaware that "POTUS" stands for President of the United States, Laurie accidentally swaps pagers with Sam, and coos with glee when he calls her—then is quite let down when she learns he just wants to swap pagers. Under close questioning from Sam, she reveals that she is indeed a hooker, but that she went to bed with him because she liked him. She has no intention of telling the press about their liaison, and reassures Sam that his career is safe with her... 2 speeches & 33 lines (3)

[MARY MARSH]   A well-groomed, middle-aged woman, she is a prominent member of the Religious Right, a spokeswoman for Christian Family Values, who was insulted by Josh during a face-to-face on *Meet the Press*. She later attends a peace conference at the White House, and takes Josh's apology with ill grace. Remarkably ignorant for a religious spokesperson, Mary can't keep the Ten Commandments clear in her head, and is accused by Toby of making an anti-Semetic remark... 2 speeches & 8 lines, 2 scenes (18)

[REVEREND AL CALDWELL]   A prominent member of the Religious Right, Caldwell is a good friend of Mary Marsh. He's also on good terms with the First Lady, and is her adviser on the topic of teen pregnancy. Offended by Josh's intemperate remarks to Mary Marsh, he leads a peace meeting at the White House with Toby and Joshua, and takes Josh courteously to task for his "hostility and contempt." After having a hard time controlling the equally intemperate remarks of his associates, Caldwell is treated to a withering display of outraged anger on the part of the President, is politely booted out of the White House, and is ordered to denounce the Lambs of Christ if he wants to ever return again... 1 speech & 9 lines, 1 scene (56)

STORYLINE: This is the story of a day in the life of the West Wing of the White House during the administration of PRESIDENT BARTLET, and the actions and decisions made by his staffers.

Defying Gravity on "Alias"

Alias

In recent seasons it has gotten more single-mindedly focused on its increasingly Byzantine secret-agent plotlines, but when it began, the ABC hit *Alias* represented an original, even bizarre hybrid: Spy thriller meets chick drama. Its lead character, Sydney Bristow, a pert college student who just happened to be a highly trained agent for a shadowy intelligence organization, would require an actress, the original 2000 Breakdown read, who would be "extremely smart, pretty, funny, likeable, athletic, and sophisticated...must be able to reveal emotional depth and vulnerability. And when the situation arises, kick ass."

Alternating with whiplash-inducing speed between Sydney's suspenseful, stunt-laden spy escapades, scored to a driving techno beat, and scenes of weepy domestic drama with her roommates and boyfriends, underscored by mellow Pottery Barn pop, *Alias* looked a lot like a unique hybrid of *Felicity* and *Mission: Impossible* (with a little bit of *Superman* thrown in—Sydney had to keep her life of international derring-do a secret from her college friends).

The *Felicity* association is easy enough to explain: The creator of *Alias*, J.J. Abrams, had previously originated the popular collegiate drama. The spy stuff, though, was a new wrinkle—one borne of dramatic boredom, in fact.

"It came about out of frustration in finding stories to write about on *Felicity*," Abrams told *Cult Times*. "Because there was no...crime or law or medicine or vampires or politics, there were no stories coming to our characters. It was a show about very sweet, romantic characters going through their college lives, so it didn't really lend itself to high drama.

"So I was just sort of joking that if Felicity were recruited by the CIA, you would suddenly have this wealth of stories you could do. And though I knew you could never do that on *Felicity*, it occurred to me that it could be another series."

To find the right Sydney would be a challenge in itself—so much so that the project went shopping for casting professionals as a "cast contingent" deal, meaning that if an acceptable lead couldn't be found, the show wouldn't go.

And to populate the forbidding, top-secret world of Sydney's covert career, Abrams would need meaty actors with what casting folks call "weight," meaning not physical girth but authority, presence, gravity.

Janet Gilmore and Megan McConnell had cast *Felicity* for Abrams, populating its ranks with a lot of attractive, emotive youngsters and sensitive adults. In the time between *Felicity*'s end and *Alias*' start date, though, the casting partners had added another important credit to their résumé: the David Kelley one-hour show *The Practice*. This influential legal drama had its share of perfectly coiffed leads, but around them was a finely culled and complementary ensemble. And, in its roster of recurring characters—judges, prosecutors, perps, rival lawyers—*The Practice* was a virtual clearinghouse of "weighty" actors, usually with reams of theatre and TV credits and the kind of seasoned acting chops that can't be faked.

Not faking was important to Abrams' conception. While the pumped-up spy scenes would have their share of incredible, even preposterous moments—indeed, precisely *because* they contained such moments—Abrams wanted his cast to play everything deadly straight.

DEFYING GRAVITY ON "ALIAS"

Recalls casting director Janet Gilmore, "[J.J.] wanted all the secret agent stuff to be believable, not like 'acting' they're secret agents."

Her partner, Megan McConnell, chimes in: "He wanted a lot of characters with weight and authority, which is why he wanted to work with us again, because he liked the casting we'd done on *The Practice*. If he had only worked with us on *Felicity* and we hadn't done that other stuff, I don't think we would have been casting this."

The project started with a six-week deal to find the right Sydney. A small group of actresses were considered for the role, among them Jacinda Barrett (*The Real World*, *The Human Stain*). "She's the only one who gave a reading who could have maybe done the part," McConnell recalls.

Except for, of course, the one who got it. Indeed, while Gilmore and McConnell did their share of searching for the perfect Sydney, it was Abrams who first suggested Jennifer Garner. Gilmore and McConnell had brought her in as a recurring love interest on the last season of *Felicity*, and while Abrams certainly remembered her work on that show, Garner's potential was recalled to him in a less conventional way.

Says McConnell, "J.J. pitched the project to us and he said, 'The only person who might be able to do it, and I'm not sure that she can, but I was just at her wedding, and she's so charismatic, she just was radiating, is Jennifer Garner.'" (Actors, take note: You're *always* auditioning, even on your wedding day.)

The network was encouraged enough by the project's progress that it quickly went from "cast-contingent" to a pilot pickup, even before the ink was dry on Garner's deal. That meant Gilmore and McConnell's work began in earnest in early 2001. Their first decision: To find those "weighty" actors, they had to go to New York. Most networks, including ABC, have casting departments on the East Coast as well as the West, but McConnell and Gilmore say they believed in the project so much that they wanted to be there themselves. This wasn't the usual practice.

"It was very unusual," says Gilmore, "to the point where we paid our own ticket, because we felt very passionate about this project. The ABC people in N.Y. are fantastic; it's not that we don't trust them, but we wanted to be part of the decision-making, because we were so attached to this project. We felt that we knew J.J. better than they would know J.J.."

Ironically, the two New York-based theatre heavyweights who ended up in the show's regular cast—Ron Rifkin and Victor Garber—didn't meet with the casting directors on their New York visit. Not for lack of trying, though: "Actually there was a horrible snowstorm, and Ron Rifkin couldn't make it in to see us," Gilmore explains. Later, in a use of technology that Sydney herself would appreciate, both Rifkin and Garber auditioned from New York by a satellite feed.

But the CDs did make at least one momentous discovery while they were in New York: a young actor named Bradley Cooper, who walked in the room to audition for the part of Clay ("a really, really nice guy," reads the Breakdown, adding "and he's cute too").

"He'd just graduated, I think the year before," McConnell recalls.

"From NYU," Gilmore adds, describing the audition of this then-unknown: "He walked in the room and read it, and it was like, Oh my God, this is absolutely the guy. It was that feeling."

As with a number of the roles on the original Breakdown, Clay's name was changed before the shoot, to Will Tippin, an intrepid investigative reporter (though presumably the "nice" and "cute" aspects still applied).

Another character that was tweaked from the original Breakdown was Larry Hirsch, described as "Mid 40s...married for 18 years...a bit of a mentor to Sydney." Abrams wasn't even sure whether Hirsch would be "regular" or "recurring" at the time.

Despite the character's Semitic name, McConnell says, "We kind of always saw that [role] as African-American." When Carl Lumbly—a Bay Area theatre actor with tons of film and TV credits—walked in, they saw a match for a part that had been, at Gilmore puts it, "hard to cast."

"Carl had just such a fatherly feel, a warmth to him—a sense of trust," Gilmore recalls. The role became Marcus Dixon, one of Sydney's colleagues at the fictional intelligence agency SD-6, and became a series regular. And while Dixon has certainly emerged as an exemplary character, the "warmth" Gilmore noted in Lumbly has often been shrouded behind a cool, self-possessed exterior.

Gilmore agrees that Lumbly has deftly embodied the secretive side of Dixon: "He has a lot of authority and experience, and you believe that he is who he is when he says who he is."

The standout comic role of Marshall, a tech geek who eagerly demonstrates the latest gadgets to Sydney and her colleagues, was described in the original Breakdown as "a mess...scraggly facial hair and messy hair...extremely intelligent, although you would never know it by looking at him...possibly overweight or out of shape."

"That part was really challenging, and we read a lot of people," McConnell says. Abrams' conception of the role was, as the Breakdown suggests, more slob than nerd. "Scientific and strange, like the guy who never shaved or took a bath or changed his clothes," Gilmore explains. "Everybody else [at SD-6] had to dress nice. He was somebody who wouldn't necessarily have to go with the same dress code, because he was such a genius that he didn't have to follow their rules."

Slightly off that track was a short, nervy actor they'd cast on *Felicity*, Kevin Weisman. He wasn't overweight, and he was more high-strung than absent-minded. Recalls McConnell, "I kinda kept asking J.J., 'Don't you remember that guy, do you wanna read him?' And J.J. kept saying, 'No, I don't see it that way.' Finally, the third time I asked him, he said, 'You know, if you have a really strong instinct about that, just bring him in.' We brought him in, and [Kevin] can just improv like crazy." Actors are often advised not to go "off script" in an audition with the writer in the room—but Weisman had the comic instincts to do his extended riff in the character of Marshall, demonstrating to Abrams his take on the loveable gearhead. "J.J. loved it," says McConnell.

Another actor who improvised during the audition process did so in a much more high-stakes situation—the kind of gambit that could cost rather than win a role. It was during the network test— an intense process in which actors read for not only the casting staff and the producers but network executives with an eye on the advertising bottom line—that theatre veteran Ron Rifkin started to improvise.

"I was reading with him," Gilmore recounts. Her reaction to Rifkin's off-book meandering? "'Aggggh! Where's he going with this?' Luckily I've done a lot of improv, so I kept up with him, and luckily he got the part, because if he hadn't, I would have always thought: My God, if I had improv-ed better with him...."

Of course, such an outcome wouldn't be entirely Gilmore's fault. For an actor to do that at the network level could be seen as either incredibly ballsy or just plain foolish.

"It came totally out of the blue," Gilmore says. "It's not like he came up to me and said, 'Is it OK if I...?' And I would have said, 'Sure.' But he didn't." Despite the momentary heart palpitations, Gilmore says, "It worked out fine." The key, as with Weisman's impromptu bits as Marshall, was that Rifkin kept his improvisations in character.

In fact, perhaps Rifkin was taking to heart the brief, enigmatic Breakdown for the quietly sinister character he plays, Arvin Sloane: "He has a powerful and magnetic presence...intelligent." What better way for Rifkin to demonstrate Sloane's perverse, manipulative power than to throw an unexpected curve ball at his network test?

Abrams has returned the favor with many of his actors in the seasons since, giving them many unexpected twists and turns. No actor has had a more deliciously challenging assignment than Merrin Dungey. Initially she played Francie, Sydney's unsuspecting college roommate, whose romantic and professional challenges were part of the show's more *Felicity*-like domestic side. In Season Two, Francie was murdered by a perfect double named Alison who took over Francie's identity to spy on Sydney. This new character, also played by Dungey, was harder, sleeker—and, to use the parlance of the original Breakdown for Sydney, expected to "kick ass."

Was this unusual character arc known at the time Gilmore and McConnell first cast Dungey in the pilot?

"No, not at all," says McConnell.

"Merrin Dungey was someone we were fans of when we were casting David Kelley's *Snoops* a couple years prior," recalls Gilmore. "She came really close [to a lead role]."

Along with Weisman, Dungey is a member of the L.A.-based Buffalo Nights Theatre Company, which has won acclaim mostly for productions of seldom-produced 20th-century work. Indeed, theatre work seems to be a common denominator among the *Alias* ensemble: Apart from Garner and Michael Vartan, who plays Sydney's sometime squeeze, Agent Vaughn, all the show's regulars have extensive theatre backgrounds.

McConnell recalls of the first "table read"—the initial gathering of the cast to read through the script around, yes, a table—that "they all bonded before the reading even started over their theatre stuff."

Theatre backgrounds have meant more to *Alias* over the years than the "weight" mentioned earlier. The versatility that the stage teaches an actor has also come in handy when the show has thrown in touches of comedy—not outright jokes, perhaps, but subtle, knowing humor based on our familiarity with the character's quirks.

Not only the nerdy Marshall but such straitlaced characters as Jack Bristow, Sydney's father, played by Victor Garber, and Rifkin's Sloane, have pulled off sly, winking moments that have displayed their expert timing. Was Abrams specifically looking for actors who, while conveying stone-faced authority, could dip into a comic palette as well?

"I think he knew Ron Rifkin has it," says McConnell. "Victor Garber has that, but I don't think that J.J. was looking for that. [Jack] was a dead serious character. And other characters were for the other part of her life, [which] was very much like *Felicity*, so their auditions lent themselves to that lighter tone."

In fact, McConnell says, under most circumstances Abrams "responds to funny. During *Felicity*, you could just know who they were going to cast by who got the most laughs from J.J. and Matt [Reeves], his partner. The two of them would crack up at something, and that person would always get the part."

TRANSITIONS AND COUPS

One incentive for casting directors to do a good job of casting a pilot, apart from building a reputation in the industry (and possibly even winning an Artios award, an honor given by their peers in the Casting Society of America), is that it can be a great audition for the job of casting the series, if it's picked up. As excited as they were about *Alias*, McConnell and Gilmore had to make a difficult lifestyle decision: Their offices until recently were on the Manhattan Beach lot Fox Studios built for David E. Kelley productions, and *Alias* was being produced by ABC, located in Burbank near the Walt Disney lot. Anyone with even the slightest familiarity with L.A. geography knows that the beaches and the Valley are separated by several freeways, a few mountains, and dozens of miles.

McConnel and Gilmore had done the commute—around an hour, if they were lucky—while working on the pilot. Both have small children and live close to Manhattan Beach. The choice was clear, if not easy.

"Casting it was a great experience, and it was really hard, frankly, to give it up," says Gilmore. "It was just about lifestyle for us. We have small kids, and we're based down here on *The Practice*. In the first year of [*Alias*], it was going to be complicated."

If, as Gilmore says, giving up casting the series was "like giving up a child," it was "important...who takes care of that child. So were we ecstatic that April [Webster] took it over."

Webster, a seasoned casting director whose other credits include the pilots of *CSI* and *Providence* and the features *The Day After Tomorrow* and *The Patriot*, has clearly kept up the standards set by Gilmore and McConnell: The three were nominated jointly for pilot and first season casting, not only by their peers in the CSA but by the Academy of Television Arts & Sciences, which started giving out Emmys for casting in 1995.

"April Webster has continued to do an amazing job of casting," raves Gilmore of her successor. "It's very stylish."

For her part, Webster returns the favor, calling Gilmore and McConnell's original cast "an incredible gift" to her. "These are people who know how to work as an ensemble, so when you bring new actors in, they don't feel left out."

Among Webster's high-profile casting coups in later seasons was tapping Lena Olin to play Sydney's long-lost mother, an enigmatic figure with complicated alliances who was thought to be dead for the first season. Though Gilmore and McConnell didn't cast Garber and Garner for their resemblance, there's an eerie perfection to this unlikely family trio. For the first season, Sydney seemed to become more and more her father's daughter—tough, secretive, uncompromising. The addition of Olin fills out not only the genetic picture but the cunning, calculating, almost feline side of Sydney.

A less noted casting discovery of Webster's is David Anders, who plays the pale, thin villain Sark. As Webster recounts, Anders first auditioned as a Russian, then as an Irishman, and finally, over the phone, as an Englishman. What's more, though the part was initially intended as a guest spot, the producers liked him so much they turned him into a major recurring player.

Casting isn't done in a vacuum, of course. The art of the TV casting director is to present the show's writer/producer with the best possible choices. The final choice—and the quality of that choice—rests with the boss. Using that standard, Gilmore and McConnell attest, there's no question why *Alias* has maintained its hit status.

"J.J. is a very strong producer who knows what he wants," says Gilmore. "He's open to stuff, and you can think out of the box and bring him something different."

"He's totally open, but he does know what he wants," McConnell adds.

"He doesn't waffle," Gilmore sums up. "If it walks in the room, he just responds."

For their part, these casting partners—who anticipate more work with Abrams in the future—feel privileged to have brought in the actors Abrams responded to.

"We knew from the moment he pitched it—I mean, he pitched it, we didn't even see a script—we were so excited," Gilmore says. "We all knew we had something special on our hands. We thought it was a little groundbreaking—not like no one's ever come up with this idea before, but for television to accomplish what J.J. accomplishes in, you know, forty-two minutes every Sunday, it's pretty impressive."

What Gilmore and McConnell accomplished in the tight schedule of 2001's busy pilot season is pretty impressive, too.

 **BREAKDOWN SERVICES, LTD.** Los Angeles New York Vancouver London   The information contained in this document is
(310) 276-9166 (212) 869-2003 (604) 943-7100 (01) 459-2781   the exclusive property of Breakdown Services,
BREAKDOWN SERVICES, LTD.   Ltd. Any unauthorized reproduction, duplication,
www.breakdownservices.com   The Link: www.submitlink.com   copying or use of the information contained
herein, without prior written consent of
Breakdown Services, Ltd., is strictly prohibited.

(File 1116p01-kfm) L

(P. 1115p02-rhm) L

TOUCHSTONE TELEVISION

"UNTITLED J.J. ABRAMS PILOT"

ONE HOUR PILOT / ABC

__DEL'D IN LA Fri., Nov 17, 2000, Vol. 2000, #1117__

Executive Producer: J.J. Abrams

Producer: TBA

Director: TBA

Writer: J.J. Abrams

Casting Directors: Janet Gilmore / Megan McConnell

Casting Associate: Jonell Dunn

Casting Assistant: Jennifer Lare

Location: TBA

Start Date: TBA

WRITTEN SUBMISSIONS ONLY TO:

GILMORE / MCCONNELL CASTING

Breakdown released Thurs., Nov. 16, 2000. Please note that this is a LINK project.

Use THE LINK/STARCASTER to submit actors immediately for this project.

PLEASE SUBMIT IMMEDIATELY, ALTHOUGH AUDITIONS WILL NOT BE SET UP UNTIL AFTER THANKSGIVING.

[SYDNEY] FEMALE, 24–28, extremely smart, pretty, funny, likeable, athletic, and sophisticated. Actress must be able to reveal emotional depth and vulnerability. And when the situation arises, kick ass …SERIES LEAD

Los Angeles (310) 276-9166 New York (212) 869-2003 Vancouver (604) 943-7100 London (01) 459-2781

BREAKDOWN SERVICES, LTD.
www.breakdownservices.com

The Link: www.submitlink.com

(File 0122p05-lkm) L
(P. 1116p01-kfm) L
(P. 1115p02-rhm) L
TOUCHSTONE TELEVISION
"ALIAS" (FORMERLY
"UNTITLED J.J. ABRAMS PILOT")
ONE HOUR PILOT / ABC

DEL'D IN LA Tue., Jan. 23, 2001, Vol. 2001, #0123
Executive Producer: J.J. Abrams
Producer: Sarah Caplan
Director: J. J. Abrams
Writer: J.J. Abrams
Casting Directors: Janet Gilmore / Megan McConnell
Casting Associate: Jonell Dunn
Casting Assistant: Jennifer Lare
Location: Los Angeles
Start Date: Approximately 3/8/01

WRITTEN SUBMISSIONS ONLY TO: GILMORE / MCCONNELL CASTING

Breakdown for the lead role of "Sydney" was released Thurs., Nov. 17, 2000.

Use THE LINK/STARCASTER to submit actors immediately for this project.

SCRIPT IS NOT AVAILABLE. PLEASE DO NOT CALL OR SEND FOR A PICKUP.

[JACK BRISTOW] Late 40s to late 50s. Sydney's father. Intelligent, intense, strong, very agile physically...SERIES REGULAR

[AGENT VAUGHN] 30s. Handsome. Charming. Strong. Potential love interest for Sydney...SERIES REGULAR

[FRANCIE] Mid 20s. Any ethnicity except Caucasian. Funny and sincere. She is a caterer, Sydney's dearest, lifelong best friend...SERIES REGULAR

[LARRY HIRSCH] Mid 40s. He has been married 18 years. He is a bit of a mentor to Sydney...SERIES REGULAR OR RECURRING GUEST STAR

[ARVIN SLOANE]   50. He has a powerful and magnetic presence. Intelligent...SERIES REGULAR

[MARSHALL]   Late 20s to late 30s. He's a mess. Scraggly facial hair and messy hair. Extremely intelligent, although you would never know it by looking at him. Possibly overweight or out of shape...SERIES REGULAR

[CLAY GIBBONS]   Late 20s to early 30s. The first thing you notice about him is that he's a really, really nice guy. He's Sydney's other best friend and confidante, and he's cute too...SERIES REGULAR

[AGENT McCOLLOCH] Early to mid 60s. Stern, smart, humorless...RECURRING GUEST STAR

[DANNY HECHT]   Mid to late 20s. Medical student. Handsome, funny, low-key...MAJOR GUEST STARRING ROLE

Who Wants to Face Reality?

On its face, the phrase "reality casting" would seem to be an oxymoron. Aren't the castaways on *Survivor*, the young suits on *The Apprentice*, and the catfighting harem on *The Bachelor* supposed to be, well, real people? How do you "cast" real people?

The industry has quickly learned the answer to the question, as reality TV has gobbled up a huge share of primetime, and as ratings for shows like *Joe Millionaire* and *Top Model* continue to batter the competition. Reality TV may not dominate the airwaves forever, but it's not going away.

For casting director Katy Wallin, this is good news. Her Burbank offices, where she's cast such scripted projects as *Mighty Morphin Power Rangers* and most recently *National Lampoon's the Trouble With Frank*, have been bustling with activity for the last two years as she's expanded her business to include reality TV. By her estimate she has now cast fourteen reality TV projects, including *Paradise Hotel* and *Who Wants To Marry My Dad?*, and worked as a casting consultant on several more.

So she's not just talking herself up when she says of her role on reality shows, "The casting director is the most important person they're going to hire, because the cast is going to make or break the success of the show. The idea is what sold it; it's the cast that's going to determine if it's going to have 12 million people watching it. There is no script; the people that are on these shows are going to drive these storylines, so they have to be the right people."

The process of finding these people bears some resemblance to casting for scripted material, but at each step along the way it departs in significant ways from business as usual. The absence of a script is the first difference.

"Reality television is about finding real people with real stories and creating your own Breakdown," Wallin explains. "You don't get a script with a specific Breakdown from a writer, so the first thing we do is we sit down with the network and the producers and we talk—let's use *Paradise Hotel*, which was a reality soap opera. We had the producers write their ideal characters, and we created a Breakdown from those: 'We're looking for an 18- to 25-year-old female all-American girl,' or, 'We're looking for a 25- to 30-year-old Wall Street guy,' whatever it is."

These Breakdowns tend to be less detailed, and less rigorous, than Breakdowns based on a script.

"These Breakdowns are just something that the producers would love [to see]," Wallin says. "But often you find and create storylines through other characters that are remarkable, because they have such unique backgrounds and profiles. It's about the mix—who is the mix of people, how are they gonna interact?"

Before she gets to mixing and matching, though, Wallin must assemble the elements. She begins by looking at a map, essentially.

"What we would do is we would look at the country and pin-point specific demographics, where we knew we could target these different people—certain colleges, maybe events that are happening," Wallin says of the typical process. "And we would go to twenty cities, and then train casting staff to go out and actually find these particular individuals."

Typically applicants are drawn to open calls by ads in local papers or on the radio. At these mass casting calls, Wallin's scouts put applicants on tape with "a pretty simple interview" and have them fill out a "very extensive application" with a "lot of personal questions on it." The tapes and applications are set to Wallin, and she and her staff review everything.

And this isn't even for the background check—this is just the first level of vetting.

"It's to get to know, who are these people? It's about their profile: What do they do, what are their likes, what are their dislikes, how do they describe themselves? We get into their emotional profile, their physical profile. And then from there we pick people who we want to call back. This is almost compared to what a pre-reading is."

In scripted film and TV casting, the "pre-read" phase is the one where the casting director auditions as many people as she can, from which she call backs her choices to present to her bosses—the director or the producers, depending on the job.

From an initial pool of thousands, Wallin winnows down the choices to several dozen—sixty to seventy-five, on average—who are then flown to Los Angeles for the final stage of the casting process. This last phase is challenging and intensive, combining the executive-level pressure of network pilot testing with a background check that rivals a White House security clearance for thoroughness.

"You sequester them in a hotel," Wallin explains. "And then an extensive process takes place, where they meet the casting director, the executive producers, a psychologist, a private investigator, a medical examiner. We have to assess the profile and history of these folks, but we also have to assess what's called risk management."

Indeed, this process, like the pitch-meeting phase of *Project Greenlight*, would probably make compelling television in itself.

"That's where we really learn who these people are; a lot comes up," says Wallin. "We get a whole profile, and then we're able to determine: Are these people going to be on an island for X amount of time? What's gonna happen to them? Are they gonna break down? You need to know that type of thing."

It shouldn't surprise anyone who's watched any reality TV that a propensity to "break down" doesn't exactly disqualify a prospective cast member. Indeed, it may be a plus—within reason.

"A lot of people on these shows have very extensive emotional histories, and that's why they create really great drama," Wallin says. "*Paradise Hotel* was like a real-life *Melrose Place*, and we needed folks that had, you know, interesting lives, because those create storylines."

Does this mean that producers actually seek people with psychological quirks, even damage, just because it makes great TV? Where do they—or Wallin—draw the line?

"I don't think they're looking for anybody who's going to harm themselves or emotionally be harmful," Wallin says. "But certainly people who have colorful emotional histories—and who are open to talking about it—are going to probably make for good reality TV."

Still, producers take the "risk assessment" part very seriously, especially since some shows that came early in the recent rush of reality shows—*Temptation Island* was one—had questions arise mid-series about their cast members' sexual past.

"The background checks have become a lot stricter because of liabilities," Wallin avers. "It's a very important component of this process." She estimates that between 30 and 40 percent of prospective cast members are eliminated due to medical, psychological, even criminal factors.

"Obviously, if you're going to put someone on a network show, you have to assess their risk," Wallin continues. "If they have a criminal history or something where it could possibly harm another individual, they're not gonna make it onto a show."

Cast members' pasts are mere prologue, though. How they fit into the group and respond to others is crucial, as well.

"Just like in the scripted world, chemistry is everything," Wallin says. "We explore the chemistry of these individuals, because if we're doing a real-life soap opera, then we need to know how these select individuals are going to interact, and most importantly *react* to each other."

Whoa—that's two words with "act" in them in one sentence. Which raises a key question about reality shows: What does their popularity means for the future of trained actors, let alone scriptwriters, directors, costume designers, costume designers, and so on—all the people typically employed by Hollywood's "Dream Factory" to create believable fictions?

There are "story producers" on reality shows, as Wallin points out—positions typically filled by writers—who help steer and shape the unscripted footage. And not all reality shows are looking for the kind of drama that seems to compete directly with scripted shows.

"I just did a home renovation show called *The Complex,* so we weren't really looking for actors, we were looking for real people who were real couples who were going to go in and renovate a home," Wallin says. "People who were great TV, great characters, auditioned for the renovation show, but their skill and their love and their hobby is renovation; they've never auditioned for another show."

But that kind of specialization isn't the case with many of the shows she's done, Wallin concedes.

"I've done a lot of relationship shows, and you tend to see a lot of people audition over and over for those," Wallin says. "There is a talent pool."

Now there's concept that's difficult to get the mind around: a "talent pool" of real people, presumably non-actors. But, as anyone who's followed a reality show featuring young, attractive cast members from urban centers who list their profession as "student," there's clearly no sign on the casting door advising actors—particularly of the aspiring variety—that they need not apply.

"On *Paradise Hotel,* a lot of those people were probably people who wanted to pursue acting—you know, it's an unscripted soap opera," Wallin says. "It really depends what type of show we're casting."

In general, though, as reality shows have tightened their grip on primetime, Wallin is seeing more and more submissions from actors—and not only of the aspiring kind.

"A lot of actors are now wanting to audition for reality," says Wallin, who says she now gets "hundreds" of submissions from agency-represented talent for reality roles. She'll often place a notice through Breakdown Services, and she says she often astonished by the response.

"I also got called to do the experts for *The Complex,*" Wallin says of the home-renovation show. "I released it in Breakdown, and it was *amazing* how many submissions we got for the real estate person, for the interior designer. I thought, 'We'll release it in Breakdown and maybe one or two submissions will come in.' We were *inundated.*"

There's another category of serial applicant: the fans, who are openly invited by the networks' websites not only to follow the shows but to show up at the frequent open calls.

"Some people are really obsessed with reality TV," Wallin says. "They really live vicariously through these shows, so they track who's casting what."

You'd think such obsession would be an automatic turnoff, but Wallin says that's not necessarily so.

"If somebody wants their fifteen minutes of fame, that person doesn't always make for the best candidate," she concedes. "But maybe they'll be the best candidate, depending on the reality show."

Those obsessional reality fans can now track their favorite cast members' post-show careers, since a part on a reality show can occasionally be the "breakout role" that advances an actor's career. *The Real World*'s Jacinda Barrett works a lot, and was even considered for a major series lead (see the chapter on *Alias*), and Wallin says she recently called in Colby Donaldson, a well-known *Survivor* alumnus, for a scripted project.

Whatever their post-show paths, it's clear that after they've appeared on a popular TV show, none of these reality TV cast members are just "real people" any more. As Wallin points out, some of Hollywood's major agencies have "reality" divisions—not to submit talent for consideration on reality shows, but to help shepherd their post-show opportunities. This has been a relatively recent phenomenon, Wallin notes.

"You know, eight months ago, people would be like, 'You can't work in reality,'" she says, dropping her voice to a conspiratorial whisper. "Now there are more agents referring people, and agents representing reality people. They're becoming brandable products."

Still, Wallin wouldn't keep getting calls to cast these projects if she didn't keep her eyes on the prize: real people and real stories. As with the casting directors who found the young musical prodigies for *School of Rock*, Wallin's job is to look off the beaten track and find those "rare birds," as *School of Rock* casting associate Janice Wilde memorably put it.

"When you do a scripted show, you put out a Breakdown and you're inundated," Wallin says of the usual process. "And with these shows, we can't rely on just releasing the Breakdown in Los Angeles. We have to create a nationwide strategy to go out and find these people. We can have 500 people show up for an open call, but it's about finding the right people. So you've got to figure where these people are going to be."

It can take some intrepid exploring to find what Wallin's really looking for: the casting equivalent of an untainted jury pool or a remote tribal village.

"My philosophy and strategy is to really create a grass-roots marketing plan where we can go to these little towns where maybe people have never seen [reality TV]," Wallin says. Do such places really exist? Well, even if the locals have seen *Survivor*, the point for Wallin is that "you want to find those wonderful people who aren't *consumed* by reality TV. So we end up going to little towns that not very many people have gone to."

Apart from the frequent flier miles, the reality casting process can produce another kind of exhaustion.

"It can be emotionally draining," Wallin admits. "You're hearing a lot of real life stories and experiences, and I feel like it's very important that I'm compassionate for people; people are revealing personal things."

It's worth the extra effort, though, since Wallin is essentially not simply auditioning actors to play roles but seeking the raw materials of a show's story.

"You can't write some of these stories," she says, marvelling. "Some of these characters are *unbelievable*." Actually, some of the "characters" she meets are quite literally unbelievable.

"I've met many pathological liars in this process—a lot," Wallins says. "And I'm like, 'I can't believed they lied!' I'm shocked—they've made up careers, money they've made, family history."

Come to think of it, pathological liars might make a good subject for a reality show—although the background check might be especially thorny.

All these considerations aside, Wallin—who still keeps one foot in traditional casting—insists that what she does for these shows *is* casting. While such talent finders as Lynne Spillman, who casts the reality powerhouse *Survivor*, don't come from a scripted casting background, Wallin does, as does her colleague Tara-Anne Johnson (*That 70's Show*, *Third Rock From the Sun*, *In Search of the Partridge Family*).

"It's casting," she says of her work for unscripted TV. "The difference is, we have to create the cast. We don't have the luxury of having the writer say, 'This is the character,' and actors come in and read the sides.

"The bottom line for our shows is, we're looking for real people with real stories. We're not hiring people to play characters."

That, of course, is precisely an actor's job description. Which means that while commercial television's fortunes, along with the those of casting directors like Katy Wallin's, may be tied to the future of reality TV, the craft and trade of acting remains, as always, quite blessedly unreal.

Casting Directions: The State of the Art

Ever noticed the list of credits at the beginning of a feature film and wondered, "Why are those jobs listed at the front when a whole phone book's worth of credits gets rolled out at the end?" Presumably the names upfront signify the most important creative contributors to a film's making: a list of stars and co-stars, the cinematographer, costumer, production designer, composer, editor, and of course—always significantly saved for last—the producers, the writers, and the director.

There's one other credit you'll see listed at the front of a film: "Casting by." Clearly, this signifies that the culling of talent for a film is recognized as a contribution as important as assembling costumes, designing a set, lighting a soundstage, or cutting a film.

Or does it? The casting director, it turns out, is the only professional in that roll call who lacks a union or a guild, and who remains ineligible for the industry's ultimate honor, the Academy Award.

At least one of those deficits may be addressed sooner rather than later, because for the last few years the Casting Society of America—a voluntary industry association that bestows its own peer-judged award, the Artios, and serves as an advocate, but not a bargaining unit, for casting directors—has been painstakingly putting its ducks in a row to demand recognition from producers. Last year the CSA joined forces with Teamsters Local 399 and began to line up support for a possible work stoppage if their demand for recognition wasn't met.

For Richard Hicks, currently president of the CSA, there are many reasons that casting directors haven't received basic working benefits or proper recognition, and the blame resides on both sides.

"There's an old joke: Everybody on a movie has two jobs, casting director and their own job," Hicks says from his modest office in a mid-Wilshire high-rise favored by casting directors. "The job does have its amorphous aspects—you're not sure whose idea what was, and when.

"I liken us to the old girlfriends. You have this really intense relationship with the actors and the producers, and then they go off and have really intense relationships with other people they make the movie with. When you go to the wrap party, they're like, 'Oh, I remember you.'"

That "Kodachrome" moment gives some inkling of the way casting is thought of—or, more to the point, *not* thought of.

"I think they forget, and also they co-opt," says Hicks. "What we do is set up the possibilities, and then they actually go create something. It's an interesting thing: To do a good job as a casting director, in my opinion, you really have to invest yourself and have it be meaningful, and then you have to let it go. Like a director of actors on a stage, you're no longer in control and it takes on a life of its own...you have to let it go."

What casting pros need to *stop* letting go of, Hicks insists, is the status they've earned—that front-title film credit, after all, only began happening in the 1980s when casting directors banded together to demand it.

"As casting people, we have not stood up for ourselves and demanded the respect...[we] have been willing to take no for an answer," Hicks concedes. Many casting directors, he notes anecdotally, are women or gay men who are "used to being nurturing, but not used to be demanding."

FANCY FIEFDOMS

He concedes that much of the industry's collective forgetfulness about the contribution of casting directors is honest confusion, fuelled in part by the way casting folks have approached their work.

"Casting kind of rose in the last twenty-five years, an era in which to be thought of as a worker is somehow in conflict with being thought of as an artist," Hicks says. "And to be thought of as a working 'union' person is not what we are; we are somehow fancier than that. But that way of thinking has led us into a tradition of each person having their own little fiefdom and being defensive, and thinking that the only things we can get from the equation are things that we scratch out of the earth ourselves."

Indeed, the CSA's union effort is not primarily about garnering respect in the abstract but more about improving basic working conditions. Hicks points out that almost all casting professionals, except for a few studio VPs, are contract employees—even, amazingly, the CDs with offices on studio lots who are casting series more or less year-round. Indeed, many casting directors often have steadier gigs than most electricians or actors, each of whom has a guild negotiating on their behalf.

"We'd like a health plan and a pension plan for the work that we do, like every other guild in this industry," Hicks says. He notes another grievance casting directors would like to see addressed: "We are the only craft—in our extensive research—[that is] sometimes responsible for our own support staff. The assistant location manager, for instance, is completely paid for by the production, but often, on lower-budget things or in television, there is a tradition of a cap for support staff [for casting]. So we pay the difference. In my head, I have to think, 'Well, I'm making this much money, but the truth is, I'm going to have to hire an assistant at $600 a week...'"

To get this professional recognition, Hicks concedes, he and the CSA board have had to do more than campaign their employers, represented by the Alliance of Motion Picture and Television Producers (AMPTP). He's had to campaign his peers, as well, to build and sustain solidarity in case a walkout is called for.

"It's like an election, in that you're looking to shore up your base and reach out to undecideds, and you're looking to discover how many people are unwilling, and whether it's a useful exercise to devote your time to trying to convince them or if that's going to be okay," Hicks says. "Because nobody in the union effort wants to lead the community off a cliff. That's not our objective. We won't make a move unless we feel strong, but I have to say, we feel strong. And part of the reason the industry has continued to say no to us is that they don't quite get that."

Hicks says the CSA's efforts make him confident that the Hollywood's producers will get it—the hard way or the easy way.

"We are asking the AMPTP for recognition, meaning the Teamsters will be recognized as our bargaining agent," Hicks says. "We have worked for about two solid years, and before that intermittently, to get about 85 to 90 percent of working casting directors who are willing to strike if we don't get recognized and get basic benefits."

Hicks says the CSA has learned from two local protracted strikes of recent years—the Screen Actors Guild's 2000 commercial strike, and the 2001 grocery workers strike—that timing and secrecy are of the essence for greatest impact.

"There is a timeline in the steering committee, but that is a very closely guarded secret," Hicks says. "Because part of the reason we think the grocery workers strike sucked, and the SAG commercial strike sucked, was because everybody knew, 'Oh my God, we have six months, four months, two months,' and employers were able to make defensive manuevers to deal with that. So what we're going to do is, if and when it needs to happen, it will happen—" Hicks snaps his fingers— "before they can make defensive moves."

Hicks knows that strikes are a last resort for good reason: For a while, at least, everybody loses.

"It would be tough on my community, it would be disastrous for Hollywood, and it would be a huge money-loser for everybody," Hicks admits. "Are we willing to risk that because friends of friends have died because they don't have health insurance? Absolutely.

"What I'm inviting people to do in this union effort is to look at things a different way; I'm inviting them to realize that if we pool our collective power and we move together, we can achieve things that we'll never achieve individually. And as in any negotiation, if you're not willing to walk away from the deal, you have no leverage."

CHANGING LANDSCAPE

A corollary, if not a prerequisite, to improving working conditions is to enhance the standing of casting directors in the industry. While the Academy of Motion Picture Arts & Sciences has told the CSA they don't want to add an Oscar for casting because "they don't want a longer show" (though that concern didn't stop the Academy from adding a Best Animated Movie category a few years ago), the Television Academy has been giving Emmys for casting since 1989. Hicks believes that wider recognition of casting directors' unique skills and instincts is long overdue, and he searches for comparisons that help illustrate his point.

"We're kind of like costume designers, in that we're like: 'Here, this is what we've made, what do you think of it? It's your call; it's your movie, it's your TV show.'" Much like a costume designer, a casting director is not hired just to sift through resumés like some kind of glorified human resources professional—but for his or her own taste and mental Rolodex of talent.

"Our currency is our design, if you will; we're kind of like landscape designers of actors. What makes a good casting director is a broad knowledge of actors, and an ability to express what is unique about them, and a personality that makes the process efficient and therefore monetarily beneficial for whoever you're doing it for. You're hired to make the right choices and to make them efficiently...to move through the storm of Hollywood and end up with the person who should have [the role]."

Though Hicks admits that the job always requires a balance between managerial and creative skills, in varying percentages, these two aspects are not mutually exclusive. Maybe that's because casting directors aren't filling just any sort of odd job but sorting through living, breathing performing artists whose creative potential they must find reliable ways to gauge—and then find ways to demonstrate for their employers.

"For me, it's about connections," Hicks says of both his job's managerial and aesthetic dimensions. "It's about that particular actor in that particular role—what nexus of meanings does it possess, and what are the possibilities of that person in that part? Because they haven't played a role like that, are they going to go further than somebody who has played it ten times? Because you know something about them personally, does that allow you insight into why it would be a good idea?"

He gives a telling illustration of how a casting director with taste and sensitivity can make a difference.

"I did this film called *Waking the Dead* about five years ago, and it was great for me, because Billy Crudup was the lead and they didn't have the female lead opposite," Hicks recalls. "I used to be an actor, so I read in auditions with everybody. Except for three or four big names—Gwyneth and whoever—everybody read; that's what [director] Keith Gordon wanted. So I was reading with all of these amazing actresses, and the vulnerability that they showed in those moments is something that, even now, when we see each other, there's a connection there because of what happened in that room."

Jennifer Connelly eventually landed the part, but one actress who came close to getting it, Amanda Peet, later got pegged as the hot babe in comedies such as *The Whole Nine Yards* and *Saving Silverman*. When Hicks was later casting the independent film *Igby Goes Down*, the role of an acerbic New York snob, originally slated for Winona Ryder, was suddenly available, and he remembered those dramatic *Waking the Dead* sessions.

"People were like, 'Amanda Peet?' But I was like, "No, you don't know—I saw her in the room.' And when she got to the audition for *Igby*, she said, 'Thank you so much, I would never have gotten it without you.' And she took to the part like a hungry person."

Ultimately, while the concrete improvements in working conditions sought by the union effort are unambiguous, Hicks says he understands why there still may be confusion about why casting directors continue to be shortchanged in terms of creative respect: "The job is so dynamic and so hard to pin down, and so rife for areas in which other people can take credit for it."

And technically, of course, a casting director doesn't literally hire anyone—the director does. So when stories later circulate about how an actor was "discovered" for a particular role, it's perhaps inevitable that the director only recalls as far back as the session in which a half dozen of the best possibilities came in to meet with him. The hundreds of "pre-reads," in which the casting director brought in every likely suspect and meticulously searched to find that best half dozen, are understandably a dimmer recollection.

Still, says Hicks, as a colleague pointed out to him, "Movies are not set decorator-contingent, they're cast-contingent. Finding the right actors is what makes the movie go."

PRODUCT CATALOG

FOR THE ACTOR

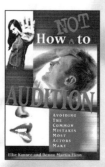

HOW NOT TO AUDITION
Avoiding the Common Mistakes Most Actors Make
by Ellie Kanner and Denny Martin Flinn

This book is mandatory reading for any actor smart enough to realize that it all starts with the audition and can easily end there as well. All great actors are unique. All bad actors are the same—they can't get through the audition to nail the job. While Kanner and Flinn can't guarantee actors a gig, they absolutely can make sure aspiring actors don't blow their auditions. Written with an edgy sense of humor, this book will steer the reader through open-calls, pre-reads, callbacks, and second callbacks.
$19.95, ISBN 1-58065-049-X

HOW TO AGENT YOUR AGENT
by Nancy Rainford

Nancy Rainford takes the reader behind the scenes to reveal the techniques, politics and unspoken rules of agenting. Agents and managers are the gatekeepers and power brokers to getting work in Hollywood. With an easy style, Rainford candidly delivers fresh insight into the mechanics and motivation of agents and managers at work. Get the tools you need to protect yourself, build a career, and train your agent to work for YOU. Filled with industry anecdotes, uncensored descriptions and accounts of show-biz players, Rainford gives you the advice and know-how you will wish you'd learned years ago.
$17.95, ISBN 1-58065-042-2

HOW TO GET THE PART... WITHOUT FALLING APART!
Featuring the Haber Phrase Technique® for Actors
by Margie Haber with Barbara Babchick, foreword by Heather Locklear

Acting coach to the stars Margie Haber has created a revolutionary phrase technique to get actors through readings without stumbling over the script. The book helps actors break through the psychological roadblocks to auditioning with a 10-step method for breaking down the scene. Actors learn to prepare thoroughly, whether they have twenty minutes or two weeks. Includes celebrity photos and audition stories.
$17.95, ISBN 1-58065-014-7

MAKING MONEY IN VOICE-OVERS
**Winning Strategies to a Successful Career in
TV, Commericals, Radio and Animation**
By Terri Apple, Foreword by Gary Owens

This book helps the actor, radio DJ, vocal impressionist and amateur cartoon voice succeed in voice-overs, no matter where they live. From assessing one's competitive advantages to creating a demo tape to handling initial sessions, Terri Apple provides a clear guide full of insider tips and strategies helpful to both beginners and experienced professionals.
$16.95, ISBN 1-58065-011-2